Interstate Apportionment of
Business Income for
State Income Tax Purposes

Interstate Apportionment of Business Income for State Income Tax Purposes

With Specific Reference to North Carolina

by

CHARLES E. RATLIFF, JR.

Chapel Hill

THE UNIVERSITY OF NORTH CAROLINA PRESS

Preface

Interest in the problem of apportioning business income for state income tax purposes has existed ever since the levy of the first successful state corporate income tax in 1911, but never before has it been so intense as today. Gradually increased concern over the years is accounted for by expansion of interstate commerce and the number of states taxing business income; however, the current extraordinarily high level of concern is primarily a result of recent Supreme Court decisions relaxing constitutional limitations on the power of states to tax income earned in interstate commerce.

This study was prompted by the existence of the problem in general and by the recent revision in the North Carolina apportionment formula. I am especially indebted to Dr. B. U. Ratchford of the Federal Reserve Bank of Richmond, who encouraged me to undertake the study and who made valuable criticisms and suggestions at various stages of the work. The study was accomplished while I was on sabbatical leave from Davidson College serving as a Research Fellow of the Inter-University Committee for Economic Research on the South. I am grateful to the committee and the college for enabling me to make the study. I also wish to express my appreciation to the committee for a generous grant to assist in the publication of this book.

To the many persons who have contributed to this

study I am deeply indebted. In the course of the investigation I have had conferences with numerous corporate
officials, state officials, political leaders, and economists,
who most graciously gave me their time. Many other
persons kindly participated in the study through corre-
spondence. The amount of time and effort required on
the part of corporations to co-operate in the study is evi-
denced by the nature and extent of the data requested
from them and presented in the following pages.

I am particularly grateful to Mr. Hudson C. Stansbury,
Director, and the other members of the North Carolina
Department of Tax Research for their helpful spirit and
the fullest co-operation legally allowable.

CHARLES E. RATLIFF, JR.

Davidson, North Carolina
July, 1961

Contents

Tables

Interstate Apportionment of Business Income for State Income Tax Purposes

Chapter I

Introduction

Objective and Scope

Within the interdependent American economy, business firms to an increasing extent operate in more than one of the states, thirty-six of which, plus the District of Columbia, levy corporate taxes on or measured by net income. Naturally in this situation problems arise regarding the jurisdiction of a state to tax a firm's net income, the definition of net income, and the determination of the portion of net income attributable to a particular state. This study deals with the last of these problems as it relates to mercantile and manufacturing corporations, with particular reference to North Carolina, which recently revised its method of apportionment.

The apportionment methods used by the thirty-six corporate income tax states and the District of Columbia vary. Differences exist with respect to permission to use separate accounting, the direct allocation of non-unitary income such as income from property unrelated to the main business, and the formulae used to apportion the unitary income. Various economic, political, and legal factors account for these differences among the states and for revisions within a state. The apportionment methods employed by the states affect decisions regarding resource allocation, the costs of complying with the tax laws on the part of corporations, and the costs of administering the laws by the states, and thus are of considerable economic significance.

The purpose of this study is to analyze the income apportionment problem generally and the case of the North Carolina revision specifically. First, the legal and economic developments are concisely reviewed. This brings together in one place a survey of the Court's interpretation of the commerce and due process clauses as they apply to state taxation of interstate commerce, the development of ideas as to the proper method for apportioning among the states the net income of a multi-state business, and the apportionment formulae used by the states. Second, the experience of North Carolina in connection with the 1957 formula revision is presented as an exemplary case. Here the primary object is to analyze the actual effects of the revision, insofar as they can be ascertained, and compare them with the expected effects. Since the new formula went into effect at midyear and taxpayers computed apportionment percentages under both the old and new formulae in 1957 returns, an exceptional opportunity is afforded for isolating the revenue effects of a formula revision. This is in sharp contrast to the usual extremely rough estimates of the revenue effects of formula changes. The case study serves in helping to develop general principles relating to a proper apportionment method and the desirability of uniformity in method among the states.[1] Third, the economic analysis of apportionment and uniformity is presented. The analysis of income apportionment leads to a suggested apportionment formula, while the analysis of uniformity includes

1. Incidentally, North Carolina was involved in the only case of a tax being declared unconstitutional because of an unreasonable apportionment formula and in one of the recent cases precipitating the current concern. These are *Hans Rees' Sons, Inc.* v. *North Carolina*, 283 U.S. 123 (1931) and *ET&WNC Transp. Co.* v. *Currie*, 359 U.S. 28 (1959), referred to in Chapters II and III.

the case, on economic grounds, for a uniform method of apportionment and consideration of methods of implementing such uniformity.

Source and Method

As indicated in the footnotes, many references were drawn upon to paint the backdrop of constitutional, economic, and statutory aspects of the problem. These include journal articles, court cases, monographs, association proceedings, Congressional hearings, state study commission reports, and tax services. The sources employed to trace the developments leading to the change in the North Carolina law include material in the files of the North Carolina Department of Tax Research, newspapers, and information obtained by interviewing individuals associated with the developments in various capacities. Most of the statistics presented in the study were obtained directly from the corporations, as indicated below, and from the North Carolina Department of Tax Research.

To help determine the effect of the revised formula on North Carolina tax revenue, certain corporations were asked to recompute their tax liabilities under the old formula and compare these with their liabilities under the new. They were also asked to show the changes in apportionment percentages and to indicate the features of the revised formula producing the change. To determine the effect on revenue of a property-payroll formula, the corporations were asked to compute 1959 tax liabilities that would have existed had this two-factor formula been in effect. The final computations requested were relative changes from 1958 to 1959 in income subject to direct allocation and income subject to apportionment by formula.

These corporations were also asked to indicate, with

reasons, their satisfaction with or reaction to the present North Carolina apportionment formula. Observations and ideas of appropriate officials regarding the importance of the tax factor in the location of economic activity and the desirability of a uniform formula were requested. The officials were invited to supply cases supporting their positions on the importance of the tax factor in location and to give reasons for desiring or not desiring a uniform apportionment formula. They were also invited to submit ideas and observations concerning the implementation of uniformity. To guard against influencing the answers, no lists of possible reasons, ideas, or observations were supplied: the answers were of the essay type and were collated for presentation in this study (Tables VII, XIII, XVI, and XXI).

The selection of the corporations invited to participate in the study was based on the membership list of the Carolinas-Virginia Chapter of the Tax Executives Institute, data published by the North Carolina Department of Revenue, and personal acquaintances. Practically all of the North Carolina TEI members, typically associated with major corporations, were interviewed personally. From the Department of Revenue publication *Stock and Bond Values* was obtained a list of widely held corporations that are taxable in North Carolina. Names and addresses of appropriate officials to be contacted were obtained from Moody's *Industrial Manual* and the North Carolina Department of Labor's *Directory of Manufacturing Firms* for firms listed therein. For others, addresses were obtained from the files of the North Carolina Secretary of State. Personal acquaintances helped in securing data from a few closely held corporations. All were assured the data would be kept confidential and

Table I

NUMBER OF FIRMS CONTACTED, REPLYING, SUPPLYING
DATA, AND REFUSING TO SUPPLY DATA,
BY METHOD OF APPROACH

Category of firms	NUMBER OF FIRMS APPROACHED BY			
	All methods	Interview	Letter to individual in firm	Letter to firm name
Contacted..............	370ª	39	219	112
Replying...............	200	39	136	25
Supplying data..........	126	31	83	12
Refusing to supply data..	51	3	38	10

ª A total of 393 were contacted, but 23 were eliminated when they replied that they were neither selling nor manufacturing businesses, or when it was determined that they were no longer in business.

the anonymity of individual corporations would be preserved.

Of the 393 corporations selected to participate in the study, 23 were eliminated because they were neither mercantile nor manufacturing firms, or were out of business. Of the remaining 370, 200 replied, 126 supplying data and 51 refusing. In general, the 23 replying, but neither furnishing data nor refusing, promised to send the data later.[2] While over half of the corporations replied to the request, only a little over a third supplied data. Undoubtedly, some of the 170 failing to reply are not mercantile or manufacturing or are out of business, so the preceding proportions are actually somewhat higher.

The results of the three methods used to acquire the data are shown in Table I. The percentages supplying data were as follows: for those interviewed, 80; for those addressed personally, 40; and for those addressed impersonally, 10. About half the interviews were with corporate officials in North Carolina and the other half with officials in New York City. For those approached

2. Inspection of data received too late to be included in the study revealed that their inclusion would not alter the conclusions.

by letter, there was one follow-up, a typed letter going to those addressed personally and a mimeographed letter to those addressed by firm name only. All of the initial letters were typed, whether addressed to an individual or to a firm.[3]

It is believed that the sample contacted is representative of the total population, but there is some bias in the results. The bias is due to the tendency of corporations receiving substantial tax relief under the formula revision to be more reluctant to divulge tax data than those experiencing substantial tax increases. A comparison of the sample results for 1957 with 1957 data compiled for the population by the North Carolina Department of Tax Research confirms this bias, as will be pointed out in Chapter IV. Because of the secrecy provision in the statutes,[4] the author could not be given access to the returns filed with the Department of Revenue or information from particular returns.

With regard to the effect of the formula revision on industrial location decisions, senior officials of 40 major corporations that have recently located or proposed the location of new or expanded facilities in North Carolina were approached by personal letter. Of the 35 replying, 33 furnished data. Details concerning this sample are presented in Chapter IV.

Organization of the Study

The study falls into three major divisions: the historical background of legal and economic aspects of apportionment (Chapter II), the North Carolina case (Chapters III and IV), and the economics of apportionment and uniformity (Chapters V and VI).

3. The letter itself was brief, requesting the firm's co-operation. Enclosed with the letter were two mimeographed sheets, one containing the questions and the other explanations of the project and the questions.

4. *General Statutes of North Carolina*, sec. 105-259.

Chapter II

Historical Background: Constitutional, Economic, Statutory Aspects

Constitutional Aspects

Due process and commerce clauses. The federal Constitution imposes several limitations on the power of states to levy taxes, the two most basic limitations being the due process clause and the commerce clause. The due process clause is a general restriction on state powers, applying only incidentally to tax powers; the commerce clause does not explicitly mention taxation, the prohibition of state taxation of interstate commerce being born of judicial implication. Briefly, the due process clause prohibits a state from taxing anything outside its jurisdiction.[1] The commerce clause delegates to the federal government power to regulate interstate commerce; however, there has been considerable division of opinion as to whether this regulatory power is exclusively federal and as to the role of the Court when state action is challenged as a violation of this clause.

COURT INTERPRETATION.[2] Even before the adoption of

1. For the purpose of the subject being studied, this statement will suffice. The clause has more specific applications to state and local taxation than the one indicated here: for example, confiscatory taxes.

2. Available are numerous sources reviewing and analyzing the legal developments in this area. Among them are Edward L. Barrett, "State Taxation of Interstate Commerce—'Direct Burdens,' 'Multiple Burdens,' or What Have You?" *Vanderbilt Law Review*, IV (April, 1951), pp. 496-532; Barrett, " 'Substance' vs. 'Form' in the Application of the Commerce Clause to State Taxation," *University of Pennsylvania Law Review*, CI (April, 1953), pp. 740-91; John R. Batt, "Death of a Salesman: New Era in Interstate Taxation," *William and Mary Law Review*, II

the due process clause of the fourteenth amendment, territorial limitations on state tax powers were recognized, based on "fundamental law" and lack of jurisdiction over the subject matter.[3] Since adoption of the amendment, such limitations have been based on due process of law. In disputed tax cases involving the state taxation of multi-state businesses, the due process and commerce clauses overlap. Taxes levied on a multi-state business for the

(June 30, 1959), pp. 223-39; John Dane, Jr., "Some Implications of Recent Supreme Court Decisions on State Taxation of Income from Interstate Commerce," *Tax Policy*, XXVI (June-July, 1959), pp. 3-11; Otha L. Gray, "State Taxation of Multi-State Corporations: Implications of Current Developments," *Atlanta Economic Review*, IX (May, 1959), pp. 3-8; Paul J. Hartman, "State Taxation of Corporate Income from a Multistate Business," *Vanderbilt Law Review*, XIII (December, 1959), pp. 21-128; Hartman, *State Taxation of Interstate Commerce* (Buffalo: Dennis, 1953); Hartman, "State Taxation of Interstate Commerce: A Survey and an Appraisal," *Virginia Law Review*, XLVI (October, 1960), pp. 1051-1120; Jerome R. Hellerstein, "Recent Developments in Commerce Clause Limitations on State Taxation," *Tax Executive*, X (January, 1958), pp. 117-40; Hellerstein, "State Franchise and Income Taxation Under the Commerce Clause," *Tax Executive*, VI (March, 1954), pp. 5-6, 20-26; Hellerstein, "State Taxation of Interstate Business Under Commerce Clause," *Journal of Taxation*, V (November, 1956), pp. 303-8; Jerome R. Hellerstein and Edmund D. Hennefeld, "State Taxation in a National Economy," *Harvard Law Review*, LIV (April, 1941), pp. 949-76; Frederic L. Kirgis, Jr., "Constitutional Law: Application of Apportioned State Net Income Taxes to Wholly Interstate Business," *California Law Review*, XLVII (May, 1959), pp. 388-95; Leonard E. Kust, "State Taxation of Income from Interstate Commerce: New Dimensions of an Old Problem," *Southwestern Law Journal*, XIV (Winter, 1960), pp. 1-22; Albert R. Menard, "State Taxation of Interstate Commerce: From Form to Substance and Back Again," *Ohio State Law Journal*, XVIII (Winter, 1957), pp. 9-21; Gilbert S. Merritt, Jr., "State Taxation of Interstate Commerce: Constitutionality of Net Income Tax on Out-of-State Corporations," *Vanderbilt Law Review*, XII (June, 1959), pp. 904-20; Dixwell L. Pierce, "Form Versus Substance," *Virginia Law Review*, XLVI (October, 1960), pp. 1150-59; Paul A. Reck, "New Court Rules on Taxation of Interstate Commerce," *Controller*, XXVII (May, 1959), pp. 215-17, 246-47; Rodman Sullivan, "Some Reflections on Taxation of Interstate Commerce," *Taxes*, XXXVIII (June, 1960), pp. 477-84. The summary presented here is based primarily on Hartman's work.

3. *Case of the State Tax on Foreign-Held Bonds*, 82 U.S. 300 (1872); *Railroad Co. v. Jackson*, 74 U.S. 262 (1868).

privilege of doing a local business, where there is no apportionment or inequitable apportionment, have been banned on both grounds. Proper apportionment, however, will enable such a tax to pass both tests.[4]

Regarding the state taxation of commerce in general, the interpretation of the commerce clause by the Court has vacillated. In the beginning there was a conflict between Marshall and Taney on the question of whether the delegation of power to Congress to regulate interstate commerce operated to restrict state action in the absence of federal action. Marshall's view was that the commerce power was vested exclusively in Congress;[5] Taney's, that the states have concurrent power to regulate interstate commerce. These two views were compromised in the *Cooley* case, which held that the commerce clause prohibits some, but not all, state regulation of interstate commerce.[6] Where the subjects of the regulation were national in character and required uniform rules of regulation, the federal power was held to be exclusive; where they were local in character, permitting diversity of regulation, state and federal powers were concurrent. Congress, under this view, could exercise complete control in both fields: it could supersede state action in local matters and permit it in national matters.[7]

The *Cooley* case did not involve a state tax, but the doctrine was later applied in the field of taxation.[8]

4. See *Hans Rees' Sons, Inc.* v. *North Carolina*, 283 U.S. 123 (1931); *International Harvester Co.* v. *Evatt*, 329 U.S. 416 (1947); *Ford Motor Co.* v. *Beauchamp*, 308 U.S. 331 (1939); Hartman, "State Taxation of Interstate Commerce: A Survey and an Appraisal," *Virginia Law Review*, pp. 1058-65.

5. *Brown* v. *Maryland*, 25 U.S. 419 (1827).

6. *Cooley* v. *Board of Wardens*, 53 U.S. 298 (1851).

7. Hartman, "State Taxation of Interstate Commerce: A Survey and an Appraisal," *Virginia Law Review*, p. 1067.

8. *Crandall* v. *Nevada*, 73 U.S. 35 (1867); *Case of the State Freight Tax*, 82 U.S. 232 (1872).

In the 1880's the Court began to employ a new test that expressed Marshall's view of exclusive federal power over interstate commerce. This was the "direct-indirect" burdens test, under which a state tax would be held invalid if it were found to be a direct burden on interstate commerce, which "cannot be taxed at all."[9] Until the 1930's the Court, in general, held that states could not tax interstate commerce under the theory that federal control over interstate commerce is exclusive, while at the same time it held, with respect to regulatory measures, that state and federal control over interstate commerce is concurrent.

The traditional views that "interstate commerce cannot be taxed at all" were scuttled in the 1930's. Chiefly responsible for replacing the old "direct-indirect" burdens test with the "cumulative burdens" test was Justice Harlan F. Stone, who had expressed his dissatisfaction with the mechanical, uncertain, remote "direct-indirect" burdens test as early as 1927.[10] Stone felt that interstate commerce should pay its fair share of state taxes and that the Court should consider, in determining the validity of a tax, its economic impact on interstate commerce. In 1938 the Court began using the "cumulative burdens" test.[11] A tax on interstate commerce would be sustained if the taxed facet of interstate commerce could not be taxed elsewhere, or, in other words, if interstate commerce was not subject to the risk of multiple taxation not borne by local commerce. Naturally, under these circumstances,

9. *Robbins* v. *Shelby County Taxing District*, 120 U.S. 489, p. 497 (1887).
10. *DiSanto* v. *Pennsylvania*, 273 U.S. 34 (1927) (dissenting opinion).
11. *Western Live Stock* v. *Bureau of Revenue*, 303 U.S. 250 (1938); *J. D. Adams Mfg. Co.* v. *Storen*, 304 U.S. 307 (1938).

apportionment methods became important considerations in the determination of tax validity.[12]

This pragmatic approach to tax validity under which state tax powers were expanded and interstate commerce paid its way was short-lived. In 1946, shortly after Stone's death, the Court resurrected the old order, holding that direct taxation of interstate commerce is in violation of the commerce clause.[13] In general, this view has been perpetuated in subsequent cases;[14] however, there are instances of a much-revised "cumulative burdens" test being used.[15]

Recently the Court has upheld net income taxes on exclusively interstate businesses.[16] The majority, in the face of strong dissents, argued that no new ground was being broken. Legal hair splitting was employed to show that "the States, under the Commerce Clause, are not allowed 'one single-tax-worth of direct interference with the free flow of commerce' "[17] and that the states cannot tax the privilege of engaging in interstate commerce, regardless of the amount of the tax or the method of apportionment.[18] Though a fairly apportioned tax levied on the privilege of engaging in exclusively interstate commerce and measured by net income is unconstitutional, a fairly

12. See *Gwin, White & Prince, Inc.* v. *Henneford,* 305 U.S. 434 (1939).

13. *Freeman* v. *Hewit,* 329 U.S. 249 (1946).

14. With respect to a privilege tax measured by net income, the Court has held that states are precluded from levying such a tax on an exclusively interstate business, regardless of the fairness of apportionment. *Spector Motor Serv., Inc.* v. *O'Connor,* 340 U.S. 602 (1951).

15. See, for example, *Memphis Natural Gas Co.* v. *Stone,* 335 U.S. 80 (1948) and *Northwestern States Portland Cement Co.* v. *Minnesota,* 358 U.S. 450 (1959).

16. *Northwestern States Portland Cement Co.* v. *Minnesota,* 358 U.S. 450 (1959); *ET&WNC Transp. Co.* v. *Currie,* 359 U.S. 28 (1959).

17. *Northwestern States Portland Cement Co.* v. *Minnesota,* p. 458, quoting *Freeman* v. *Hewit,* 329 U.S. 249 (1946).

18. *Spector Motor,* 340 U.S. 602 (1951).

14   INTERSTATE APPORTIONMENT

apportioned tax levied directly on the net income of a business engaged in exclusively interstate commerce is constitutional. The economic effect of the two may be identical, but legally they are quite distinct.[19]

Another distinction maintained by the Court is that between a tax on gross income and one on net income. It has pointed out that the former affects each transaction in proportion to its magnitude, regardless of profitability, while the latter does not arise unless there is a profit.[20] The former then is more inimical to free interstate commerce.

As for apportionment formulae, the Court has been fairly liberal in upholding any reasonable formulae against objections raised under the commerce and due process clauses.[21] In only one case has a tax been declared unconstitutional because of an unreasonable apportionment formula.[22]

The foregoing jurisdictional problems relating to state taxation of the net income of corporations are limited to foreign corporations, for the jurisdiction of a state over a corporation domiciled therein is sufficient to enable the state to tax its entire net income, including income earned outside the state, without violating the due process clause.[23]

19. Paul J. Hartman's reaction: "The guiding principle for resolving the important issue of whether a sovereign state has constitutional power to supply essential revenue needs thus turns on a judicially spawned distinction that has about as much substance as soup made from the shadow of an emaciated sparrow." "State Taxation of Interstate Commerce: A Survey and an Appraisal," *Virginia Law Review*, p. 1100.
20. See *U.S. Glue Co.* v. *Town of Oak Creek*, 247 U.S. 321 (1918).
21. See *Underwood Typewriter Co.* v. *Chamberlain*, 254 U.S. 113 (1920); *Bass, Ratcliff & Gretton, Ltd.* v. *State Tax Comm'n*, 266 U.S. 271 (1924); *Norfolk & W. Ry.* v. *North Carolina*, 297 U.S. 682 (1936).
22. *Hans Rees' Sons, Inc.* v. *North Carolina*, 283 U.S. 123 (1931).
23. *Maguire* v. *Trefry*, 253 U.S. 12 (1920); *Lawrence* v. *State Tax Commission*, 286 U.S. 276 (1932); *New York* v. *Graves*, 300 U.S. 308 (1937).

In summary, the approach of the Court to commerce clause questions throughout most of its history has been mechanical and formalistic, rather than based on substantive economic considerations. Labels and names have been more important than economics. The results, to say the least, are confusing.

CONGRESSIONAL ACTION. Congress possesses the power under the commerce clause to define the extent to which states may tax interstate commerce without adversely interfering with the national economic welfare, but until 1959 it had taken no action along this line. As shown above, it was left to the Court to make decisions in this area, and these decisions—each dealing with an isolated case—have not resulted in broad principles that will assure that interstate commerce, relative to local commerce, is neither penalized nor favored with regard to taxes. In 1959, as a result of the furor created in the business world by the *Northwestern-Stockham* and *Currie* decisions,[24] Congress acted with dispatch to hold hearings and pass a law limiting the scope of the decisions.[25] The Court held that a state may levy a fairly apportioned net income tax on a foreign corporation engaged exclusively in interstate commerce provided that the tax is nondiscriminatory

24. *Northwestern States Portland Cement Co.* v. *Minnesota,* 358 U.S. 450 (1959); *Williams* v. *Stockham Valves and Fittings, Inc.,* 358 U.S. 450 (1959); *ET&WNC Transp. Co.* v. *Currie,* 359 U.S. 28 (1959).

25. "State Taxation of Interstate Commerce—1959," *Hearing Before the Select Committee on Small Business, United States Senate* (86th Congress, 1st Session, Parts 1, 2, and 3, 1959); "State Taxation of Interstate Commerce," *Hearings Before the Committee on Finance, United States Senate* (86th Congress, 1st Session, 1959); U.S. Senate Select Committee on Small Business, *State Taxation of Interstate Commerce* (Senate Report No. 453, 86th Congress, 1st Session, 1959); U.S. Senate Committee on Finance, *State Taxation of Income Derived from Interstate Commerce* (Senate Report No. 658, 86th Congress, 1st Session, 1959); Public Law 86-272, *United States Statutes at Large,* Vol. LXXIII, pp. 555-56, amended with respect to the study referred to in the next paragraph by Public Law 87-17, *ibid.,* Vol. LXXV, p. 41.

and that there is sufficient nexus to satisfy due process. In the cases decided, the corporations maintained sales offices in the states levying the taxes; in two other cases, which the Court refused to review, sellers' agents constituted the connection.[26] Congress stipulated, however, not the activity that constitutes sufficient nexus, but that which does not: a net income tax is prohibited if the only activity within the state is solicitation of orders for tangible personal property, which orders are subject to approval outside the state and are filled by shipment or delivery from a point outside the state.

The act provided for further study of the problem for the purpose of arriving at recommendations for proposed legislation providing uniform standards to be observed by the states in imposing income taxes on multi-state businesses. In 1961 the study was expanded to include all matters pertaining to state and local taxation of interstate commerce.[27]

CONCLUSION. Regarding the taxation of the net income of corporations, the following generalizations may be made. First, a state may tax the entire net income of a domestic corporation, regardless of whether some of the income is earned outside the state. Second, a state may levy a fairly apportioned, nondiscriminatory net income tax on a foreign corporation, even if all the income is derived from interstate commerce, assuming sufficient nexus. Third, a state may not levy a privilege tax measured by net income on a foreign corporation engaged in exclusively interstate commerce or on the interstate portion of net income of one engaged in both intrastate and interstate commerce.

26. *International Shoe Co.* v. *Fontenot,* 359 U.S. 984 (1959); *Brown-Forman Distillers Corp.* v. *Collector of Revenue,* 359 U.S. 28 (1959).
27. See n. 25 above, and "Study of State Taxation of Interstate Commerce," *Congressional Record,* Vol. CVII, Part IV (March 27, 1961), pp. 4875-76.

Economic Aspects

INTRODUCTION. While the literature dealing with the legal and accounting aspects of the interstate apportionment of business income is quite extensive, that dealing with the strictly economic aspects is very limited. Of course, in the development of ideas concerning an appropriate apportionment formula and in the history of efforts to obtain a uniform formula, some underlying economic ideas may be found.

NTA PROPOSALS. For over forty years the National Tax Association has dealt with the apportionment problem, its efforts being directed principally towards obtaining agreement on a single formula to be used by all the states that tax business income.

In 1919 an NTA committee presented a model plan for state and local taxation in which business would be subject to only one business tax at the state and local level: a net income tax. The committee realized that in the case of interstate concerns the proportion of income earned within each state would have to be determined, but it envisioned no serious difficulty here.[28] The apportionment formula included in the model tax bill consisted of two factors, tangible property and gross receipts, weighted two-thirds and one-third, respectively.[29] However, a special committee appointed to consider the apportionment formula for mercantile and manufacturing businesses recommended a different formula: tangible

28. "But there are practicable methods of making such a determination, so that no serious difficulty need arise at this point." Charles J. Bullock, "Preliminary Report of the Committee Appointed by the National Tax Association to Prepare a Plan of a Model System of State and Local Taxation," *Proceedings of the National Tax Association* (1919), p. 454.

29. Charles J. Bullock, "Drafts of Personal Income and Business Income Tax Acts, Prepared for the National Tax Association by the Committee Appointed to Prepare a Plan for a Model System of State and Local Taxation," *Bulletin of the National Tax Association*, VI (January, 1921), pp. 117-18.

property and business, each weighted 50 per cent. The
business factor consisted of purchases of labor and materials and receipts from sales, the idea being that business
activity is measured by income and outgo.[30] The committee believed that this formula was more likely to be
universally adopted, since it took into account existing
legislative practices and thus was a possible compromise
between "manufacturing" states and "merchandising"
states.[31]

A third committee, appointed in 1925, found that the
property-business formula had not won universal approval,
but after several years of study and reporting it did not
recommend a particular formula. The committee stated:
"No committee, however learned in the principles of
accounting and of constitutional law, should at this time
recommend an allocation fraction unless it has first ascertained the experiences of administrators and taxpayers
with allocation fractions now in use."[32] To accomplish
this would require, in the minds of the committee, an
operation similar to that undertaken by a Congressional
committee conducting an investigation into a proposed
tariff schedule.

A fourth committee, appointed in 1929, recommended
in its final report (1933) the three-factor Massachusetts
formula, comprised of property, payroll, and sales. Argu-

30. Wage and salary payments would be assigned to the place where
the employee chiefly works or from which he operates; purchases and
sales, to the place where they are chiefly negotiated and executed. Carl
S. Lamb, "Report of Committee on the Apportionment Between States
of Taxes on Mercantile and Manufacturing Business," *Proceedings of the
NTA* (1922), pp. 198-215.

31. "Manufacturing" state refers to a state in which manufacturing
predominates over merchandising; "merchandising," vice versa. To
maximize revenue, the former tends to emphasize property in the formula;
the latter, sales.

32. Charles W. Gerstenberg, "Report of Committee on Standardization and Simplification of the Business Taxes," *Proceedings of the NTA*
(1929), p. 161.

ing that "uniformity is preferable to scientific accuracy," the committee concluded that this formula "afforded the best meeting ground for uniformity among the states."[33]

A fifth committee, presenting its final report in 1939, agreed that a property-payroll-sales formula would be best from the viewpoint of attaining uniformity, but introduced a new definition of the sales factor. The committee emphasized that the function of an apportionment formula is to locate the economic effort that produces net income. It concluded that deviation from this principle was a principal source of difficulty in defining the sales factor: "too often the situs of sales is determined as though the sale itself were being taxed."[34] Applying the principle in an analysis of various definitions of the sales factor, the committee accepted only two definitions: (1) the state to which goods are shipped and (2) the state from which the salesmen making the sales function. It recommended that half of each sale be apportioned in accordance with (1) and half in accordance with (2). The committee rejected a purchases factor primarily on the grounds that it is too easily manipulated and thus would drive the taxpayer to "uneconomic devices."[35]

Still another committee, the sixth, favored in its final report (1951) the three-factor formula.[36] Some refinements were presented in connection with the property and payroll factors, but the major change concerned the sales

33. Franklin S. Edmonds, "Report of Committee on Uniformity and Reciprocity in State Taxing Legislation," *Proceedings of the NTA* (1933), pp. 261, 262.

34. Leo Mattersdorf, "Report of the Committee of the National Tax Association on Allocation of Income," *Proceedings of the NTA* (1939), p. 209.

35. *Ibid.*, p. 194. For businesses rendering personal services, the committee recommended a two-factor formula: payroll and gross receipts, weighted 50-50 (*ibid.*, pp. 217-18).

36. Jack R. Miller, "Final Report of the Committee on Tax Situs and Allocation," *Proceedings of the NTA* (1951), pp. 456-65.

factor. The committee adopted a definition of sales that represented a compromise between the "destination" and "business activity" theories, that precluded double allocation of sales, and that insured the allocation of all sales. In general, sales would be apportioned on the basis of destination, but in the case of sales not directly or indirectly attributable to the taxpayer's activities in the state of destination they would be apportioned on the basis of origin. This was designed primarily to prevent the apportionment of income to a "no man's land," or to a state without jurisdiction to tax.

A seventh committee, reporting in 1958, found that "the only progress apparently made towards uniformity in the taxation of corporations by the state was the uniform result, that nothing came of any reports so submitted."[37] Convinced that repetitive findings would not improve the results, the committee suggested a different approach to the goal of uniformity. It was suggested that, rather than attempting to attain the goal throughout the country at the same time, the states be divided into regional districts and the governors send representatives to regional conferences having as their objective the uniform state taxation of corporate income. The following year the committee reported that, in light of the *Northwestern-Stockham* decisions and the impending Congressional study, the matter had become an urgent national issue and therefore regional efforts were discontinued. It proposed that the committee be continued and authorized to confer and work with the Congressional committees and other groups with respect to the problem.[38] In 1960 the committee, pointing to the desirability of uniformity

37. Walter W. Walsh, "Report of Committee on Interstate Allocation of Business Income," *Proceedings of the NTA* (1958), p. 373.

38. Fred L. Cox, "Report of Committee on Interstate Allocation of Business Income," *Proceedings of the NTA* (1959), pp. 223-25.

and the demonstrated futility of obtaining voluntary agreement among the states, endorsed federal action in the area and suggested the NCCUSL's proposed formula as "the framework within which Congress can provide satisfactory and effective uniformity for the allocation and apportionment of multistate income."[39]

NCCUSL PROPOSAL. The National Conference of Commissioners on Uniform State Laws, on the basis of findings of its own and of other groups, in 1957 drafted the Uniform Division of Income for Tax Purposes Act and recommended it for enactment in all states.[40] The act, approved by the Council of State Governments and the American Bar Association, incorporates the principle of a three-factor formula using property, payroll, and sales, the one to which opinion is favorable and the one towards which the states have been moving.

Giving rise to more controversy than any other feature of the act is the sales factor. Sales are allocated on the

39. Fred L. Cox, "Interim Report of Committee on Interstate Allocation of Business Income," *Proceedings of the NTA* (1960), p. 364.

40. There is an abundance of literature concerning the act. See, for example, Charles F. Conlon, "The Apportionment of Multistate Business Income: The NCCUSL Uniform Division of Income Act," *Tax Executive*, XII (April, 1960), pp. 220-35; Fred L. Cox, "Uniform Allocation and Apportionment of Multistate Income," *Tax Executive*, X (January, 1958), pp. 141-48; John Dane, Jr., "What is the Future of Public Law 86-272?" *Proceedings of the NTA* (1960), pp. 192-200; Arthur D. Lynn, Jr., "The Uniform Division of Income for Tax Purposes Act Re-examined," *Virginia Law Review*, XLVI (October, 1960), pp. 1257-68; Lynn, "Uniform Division of Income for Tax Purposes Act," *Ohio State Law Journal*, XIX (January, 1958), pp. 41-53; "New Uniform Act for Dividing Income Between States Approved," *Taxes*, XXXV (August, 1957), pp. 631-33 (complete text of act); William J. Pierce, "Uniform Act Urged as Practical Method to Lighten State Tax Compliance Burden," *Journal of Taxation*, XII (February, 1960), pp. 83-85; Pierce, "Uniform Division of Income for State Tax Purposes," *Taxes*, XXXV (October, 1957), pp. 747-50, 780-81; Walter W. Walsh, "Interim Report of Committee on Interstate Allocation of Business Income," *Proceedings of the NTA* (1957), pp. 339-41; John A. Wilkie, "Uniform Division of Income for Tax Purposes," *Taxes*, XXXVII (January, 1959), pp. 65-73.

destination basis, except in the limited situations where the federal government is the purchaser or where the purchaser is located in a state where the taxpayer's business activities are insufficient for the taxpayer to be subject to an income tax. In these limited situations, allocation is on the origin basis. Because the word "taxable" in the act is given an unusual or artificial meaning, there exists a common misunderstanding: this is that the act insures that 100 per cent of the taxpayer's income will be taxed. The act considers a taxpayer to be "taxable" in another state (1) if he is actually subject to an income tax there or (2) if that state has jurisdiction to subject him to an income tax, regardless of whether or not it has done so.[41] Therefore, sales may be allocated to a state that does not levy an income tax, and in such a situation less than 100 per cent of the taxpayer's income would be taxed under state income taxes.[42]

The NCCUSL recommended the destination basis for the sales factor for the following reasons: (1) with the origin basis the sales factor tends to duplicate the property and payroll factors; (2) with the destination basis there is less opportunity for manipulation of sales operations merely for tax avoidance; (3) some recognition should be given the state providing the market.[43] It is argued that these are, in general, the reasons for having a sales factor

41. Section 3 of the act.
42. Section 16 of the act provides: "Sales of tangible personal property are in this state if: (a) the property is delivered or shipped to a purchaser, other than the United States government, within this state regardless of the f.o.b. point or other conditions of the sale; or (b) the property is shipped from an office, store, warehouse, factory, or other place of storage in this state and (1) the purchaser is the United States government or (2) the taxpayer is not taxable in the state of the purchaser."
43. William J. Pierce, "Uniform Act Urged as Practical Method to Lighten State Tax Compliance Burden," *Journal of Taxation*, XII (February, 1960), p. 84.

in the first place; therefore, the sales factor must logically be on the destination basis.[44]

Criticism of the property factor in the NCCUSL act centers around the inclusion of rented property (at eight times the net annual rental rate) and the valuation of owned property at original cost. Proponents of the act argue that without recognition of rented property the apportionment of income would be distorted and that the use of book value for owned property, admittedly more convenient, may distort the relative contributions of old and new facilities. Criticism of the payroll factor is negligible, the taxpayer generally being able to use the same basic data for both the payroll factor and unemployment compensation tax purposes.

OTHER PROPOSALS AND SUGGESTIONS. Acceptance of the three-factor formula has been wide, but by no means universal. There are those, particularly among economists, who object to this formula on theoretical and practical grounds.

A proposal made in 1930 would apportion income on the basis of the total annual expenses incurred in each state. Capital investment would be included in expenses by being translated into equivalent annual charges at the standard rate of interest.[45] The proponent argued that it was scientifically accurate from both the legal and economic viewpoints and that it was simple. One who evaluated the idea pointed out that it might be objectionable to "market" states because a small amount of the expenses are incurred there relative to those incurred in the state of manufacture; that the accounting procedure is complex compared with the simpler, but more arbitrary, method of

44. See Conlon, "The Apportionment of Multistate Business Income," *Tax Executive*, pp. 229-30.

45. Mayne S. Howard, "Elimination of Double Taxation of Corporate Net Income," *Tax Magazine*, VIII (September, 1930), pp. 329-31.

fractional apportionment; that the whole question of
property valuation for tax purposes is involved; and that
the advocate of separate accounting might suggest that
if a detailed allocation is made of expenses a detailed
allocation of revenues should also be made "and thereby
eliminate the controversial allocation of taxable income to
a state in which no net income is earned."[46]

The separate accounting method, as the name implies,
permits a firm to treat its business in a state as if it were
separate and distinct from the business carried on outside
the state.   Proponents of the method contend that it is
more accurate than apportionment formulae.   But as a
method to be used in general by unitary business it is
theoretically and practically unsound.   Where the business within a state is truly separate and distinct from the
business without the state, separate accounting is sound,
but for a unitary business it is unsound except possibly as
an alternative in special cases where the statutory formula
is clearly inequitable.   Among the numerous objections
to separate accounting that have been voiced are the in-
consistency with economic unity, no profit being realized
until the final sale; the arbitrariness of allocating gross
income and certain expenses; the difficulties of setting
intrafirm transfer prices; expense of administration, as,
for example, higher state auditing costs; and the high cost
of compliance.[47]

46. Robert S. Ford, *The Allocation of Corporate Income for the
Purpose of State Taxation*.   Special Report of the State Tax Commission,
No. 6 (Albany: State of New York, 1933), pp. 111-13.

47. For detailed analyses, see George T. Altman and Frank M.
Keesling, *Allocation of Income in State Taxation* (Chicago: Commerce
Clearing House, 1946), pp. 37-38, 89-97; John A. Wilkie, *Allocation of
Multistate Income Under State Corporate Net Income Taxes* (Ann
Arbor: University Microfilms, Inc., 1957), pp. 137-72; Albert H. Cohen,
*Apportionment and Allocation Formulae and Factors Used by States in
Levying Taxes Based on or Measured by Net Income of Manufacturing,
Distributive and Extractive Corporations* (New York: Controllership

Included in an article that received some attention in 1939[48] was the proposal that property should not be included as a factor in the apportionment formula.[49] The argument was that the use of property, not the ownership, produces income; therefore, the profit and loss picture is best reflected by "manufacturing costs, salaries, selling costs, and gross receipts."[50]

A suggestion that has been given serious attention, at least by economists, is that a two-factor property-payroll formula is superior to the three-factor property-payroll-sales formula.[51] It is argued that income is produced by human effort and the use of land and capital, not by selling and purchasing except to the extent that human effort and property are involved in these functions. The contribution of the selling function is measured not by the volume of sales but by the outlay for labor and property performing the function. Inclusion of a sales factor in effect gives a disproportionately large weight to the labor and property involved in the selling function; in other words, it

Foundation, 1954), pp. 6-13; Ford, *Allocation of Corporate Income*, pp. 31-34, 113-15; Charles W. Gerstenberg, "Allocation of Business Income," *Proceedings of the NTA* (1931), pp. 301-32.

48. See Mattersdorf, "Report . . . on Allocation of Income," *Proceedings of the NTA* (1939), p. 191.

49. L. M. McBride, "Jurisdictional Aspects of State Income Taxation," *Taxes—The Tax Magazine*, XVII (April, 1939), pp. 197-99, 238-46.

50. *Ibid.*, p. 245.

51. C. Lowell Harriss, "Interstate Apportionment of Business Income," *American Economic Review*, XLIX (June, 1959), pp. 398-401; Harriss, "Economic Aspects of Interstate Apportionment of Business Income," *Taxes*, XXXVII (April, 1959), pp. 327-28, 361-63; Paul Studenski, "Federal Limitations on State Taxation of Interstate Commerce: An Economist's View," *Proceedings of the NTA* (1959), pp. 435-41; Studenski, "State Taxation of Interstate Commerce," *Tax Review*, XX (July, 1959), pp. 25-28; Studenski, "The Need for Federal Curbs on State Taxes on Interstate Commerce: An Economist's Viewpoint," *Virginia Law Review*, XLVI (October, 1960), pp. 1121-49; Arthur B. Barber, "A Suggested Shot at a Gordian Knot of Income Apportionment," *National Tax Journal*, XIII (September, 1960), pp. 243-51.

seems to be based on the theory that labor and property devoted to selling are more productive than labor and property devoted to other functions. Furthermore, this attribution is made to the location of a single step in the selling process: for example, the destination of the shipment, the origin of the shipment, or the location of order approving. Since property, being measured in terms of capital values rather than annual payments, and labor, being measured in terms of payments or payrolls, are computed on different bases, the weight to be given each fraction when the two are combined must be selected. Though weighting them equally may be acceptable, a labor-property ratio of two-to-one has been tentatively suggested by one economist.[52]

The property-payroll formula is advanced as the one likely to have the least tendency to distort economic decisions and adversely affect the free flow of commerce and economic growth. One practitioner, after noting the different definitions of the sales factor and their effects, has suggested that the elimination of the sales factor "may very well produce a reasonable basis for compromise of the opposed positions of the producing and consuming states."[53] An attorney argues that "there is no such thing as a 'producing state' or 'market state,'" no state being able to "import more than it can pay for with its exports."[54] Another condemns states for emphasizing the sales destination factor to "rig" apportionment formulae in

52. Harriss, "Interstate Apportionment of Business Income," *American Economic Review*, p. 401.
53. Barber, "A Suggested Shot," pp. 247-51. He notes that generally the manufacturing states, in their formulae, place emphasis on the origin or order approval bases for sales, and the consuming states emphasize the destination or solicitation bases.
54. Donald K. Barnes, "Prerequisites of a Federal Statute Regulating State Taxation of Interstate Commerce," *Virginia Law Review*, XLVI (October, 1960), pp. 1277-78.

favor of home industry and against out-of-state industry.[55] And an economist concludes: "Destination of the sales should be the basis for the imposition of state sales taxes and not for the levy of state income taxes on the selling corporations."[56]

Vehement objections, particularly by some tax administrators, are raised against the idea that the sales factor should be eliminated. It is alleged that without the market there would be no income to be taxed and that the contribution of the market is so great that it should have "a greater consideration in apportionments than has heretofore been given it."[57] The out-of-state corporation selling within a state is viewed as an "exploiter" of the state's market.[58] An economist, emphasizing that net income—not activity—is being taxed, argues for the inclusion of a destination sales factor on the ground that income of the seller is dependent upon the buyer's effective demand,

55. Floyd E. Britton, "State Taxation of Extraterritorial Value: Allocation of Sales to Destination," *Virginia Law Review*, XLVI (October, 1960), pp. 1160-71; Britton, "Taxation Without Representation Modernized," *Proceedings of the NTA* (1960), pp. 184-90; Britton, "Taxation Without Representation Modernized," *Taxes*, XXXVIII (August, 1960), pp. 628-49; Britton, "The Sales Factor in Apportioning Taxable Value of Nonresident Businesses—Allocation of Sales to Destination," *Proceedings of the NTA* (1959), pp. 428-34.

56. Studenski, "Federal Limitations," *Proceedings of the NTA* (1959), p. 440.

57. Fred L. Cox, "The Interstate Tax Problem," *Taxes*, XXXVIII (May, 1960), p. 422. See also Conlon, "The Apportionment of Multistate Business Income," *Tax Executive*, pp. 229-30; Lynn, "The Uniform Division of Income," *Virginia Law Review*, p. 1267; George H. Kitendaugh, "Possibilities for Interstate Cooperation in the Area of Allocation Formulas," *Federal-State-Local Tax Correlation* (Princeton: Tax Institute, 1954), pp. 205-10. Kitendaugh favors the destination sales factor as ideal in theory, but suggests as a practical compromise a sales factor based 50 per cent on origin and 50 per cent on destination. A 50-50 definition such as this has been recommended by a New York tax study committee (*Interim Report of New York State Tax Structure Study Committee* [1960], pp. 79-81).

58. See Cox, "The Interstate Tax Problem," *Taxes*, pp. 422-23 and Cox, "Uniform Allocation," *Tax Executive*, pp. 146-47.

which is dependent upon certain services provided by the buyer's state government.[59]

Economists might be expected to argue that income should be apportioned on the basis of the location of equity capital—on the theory that net income is attributable to such capital, other factors receiving their marginal products. Without evaluating the theory on which this conclusion would rest, one economist refrains from advancing it because he sees "no basis . . . for apportioning a firm's equity capital among states except on a basis no less arbitrary than involved in the more conventional proposal made here [property-payroll formula]."[60]

CONCLUSION. A great diversity of opinion and thinking exists among the lawyers, accountants, tax administrators, and economists who have given their attention to the problem of interstate apportionment of income. Differences in theories account for part of this diversity, but it seems that a greater part is accounted for by practical, political considerations. For the apportionment of unitary business income, the formula method over the separate accounting method is very widely accepted, but consideration of the sales factor in a formula opens Pandora's box, indeed.

Statutory Aspects

The trend in the type of formulae used by the states to apportion business income has been definitely toward a three-factor formula comprised of property, payroll, and sales or a variant thereof comprised of property, manufacturing cost, and sales, as is shown in Table II. Whereas

59. John A. Wilkie, "Corporate Tax Allocation in Wisconsin," *Land Economics*, XXXV (August, 1959), pp. 260-61. See also Wilkie, "Interstate Apportionment of Business Income," *Taxes*, XXXIX (April, 1961), pp. 354-57. For a detailed analysis, see Wilkie, *Allocation of Multistate Income*, pp. 250-65.

60. Harriss, "Interstate Apportionment," *American Economic Review*. p. 401.

Table II

APPORTIONMENT FORMULAE USED BY THE STATES AND THE
DISTRICT OF COLUMBIA, BY TYPE, 1929, 1948, AND 1960

Formula	NUMBER OF STATES USING IN		
	1960	1948	1929
Three-factor:			
Property-payroll-sales..............	24	15	2
Property-manufacturing cost-sales.....	6	5	1
Total three-factor...............	30	20	3
Two-factor:			
Property-sales.....................	2	4	1
Property-business factor.............	1	2	1
Manufacturing cost-sales.............	1	—	—
Property-manufacturing cost.........	—	3	—
Property-payroll...................	—	—	1
Total two-factor................	4	9	3
One-factor:			
Sales............................	3	3	2
Manufacturing cost................	—	1	1
Property..........................	—	—	4
Total one-factor................	3	4	7
No formula.......................	—	—	3ª
Grand total.....................	37	33	16

Source: Adapted from Prentice-Hall, Inc., *State and Local Tax Service*, pp. 1039-40, dated June 7, 1960; Leonard L. Silverstein, "Problems of Apportionment in Taxation of Multistate Business," *Tax Law Review*, IV (January, 1949), pp. 222-58; Charles W. Gerstenberg, "Report of Committee on Standardization and Simplification of the Business Taxes," *Proceedings of the NTA* (1929), pp. 163-71. Where different formulae are provided by a state for different types of business, the one shown here is for the group that includes manufacturing.

ª One (Montana) provided for separate accounting, with gross income used to allocate certain expenses. Two (Georgia and Oregon) authorized the tax commissioner to adopt regulations.

in 1929 only a fifth of the corporate net income tax states used these three-factor formulae, by 1948 the proportion was approaching two-thirds, and now it is four-fifths.

Table III identifies the states employing the various formulae. Uniformity does not exist to the degree, however, that the table may suggest, for the factors are de-

INTERSTATE APPORTIONMENT

Table III

FACTORS USED IN APPORTIONMENT FORMULAE, BY STATE, 1960

State	Number of factors	Factors Used				
		Property	Payroll	Sales	Mfg. cost	Business[a]
Alabama..........	3	x	—	x	x	—
Alaska............	3	x	x	x	—	—
Arizona..........	3	x	x	x	—	—
Arkansas.........	2	—	—	x	x	—
California........	3	x	x	x	—	—
Colorado.........	2	x	—	x	—	—
Connecticut.......	3	x	x	x	—	—
Delaware..........	3	x	x	x	—	—
District of Columbia	1	—	—	x	—	—
Georgia...........	3	x	x	x	—	—
Hawaii............	3	x	x	x	—	—
Idaho.............	3	x	x	x	—	—
Iowa..............	1	—	—	x	—	—
Kansas...........	3	x	—	x	x	—
Kentucky.........	3	x	x	x	—	—
Louisiana.........	3	x	x	x	—	—
Maryland.........	3	x	x	x	—	—
Massachusetts.....	3	x	x	x	—	—
Minnesota........	3	x	x	x	—	—
Mississippi........	3	x	x	x	—	—
Missouri..........	1	—	—	x	—	—
Montana..........	3	x	x	x	—	—
New Jersey........	3	x	x	x	—	—
New Mexico.......	3	x	—	x	x	—
New York.........	3	x	x	x	—	—
North Carolina.....	3	x	x	x	—	—
North Dakota.....	2	x	—	—	—	x
Oklahoma.........	3	x	—	x	x	—
Oregon............	3	x	x	x	—	—
Pennsylvania......	3	x	x	x	—	—
Rhode Island......	3	x	x	x	—	—
South Carolina.....	3	x	x	x	—	—
Tennessee.........	3	x	—	x	x	—
Utah..............	3	x	x	x	—	—
Vermont..........	3	x	x	x	—	—
Virginia[b]........	2	x	—	x	—	—
Wisconsin.........	3	x	—	x	x	—

Source: Adapted from Prentice-Hall, Inc., *State and Local Tax Service*, pp. 1039-40, dated June 7, 1960.
[a] Takes into consideration payroll, purchases, and sales.
[b] Effective January 1, 1962, Virginia's formula will be property-payroll-sales.

fined variously by the states. For example, among the locations to which sales are assigned are the locations of the following: office where negotiated, property at time of order, receipt or acceptance of order, negotiating personnel, point of delivery, and origin of shipment. Among the bases for allocating payrolls are: office location, time spent in the state, and compensation earned in the state.

Generally the states provide for the direct allocation of certain types of income, such as capital gains, rents, royalties, dividends, and interest. However, 6 of the 37 make no provision for the direct allocation of any income.[61] Usually states allow separate accounting in cases where the taxpayer shows that it more clearly reflects the income attributable to the state than does the formula, but again there are 6 that do not allow it.[62]

61. Alabama, Hawaii, New Jersey, Rhode Island, Vermont, and Virginia. *State and Local Tax Service* (Englewood Cliffs, N.J.: Prentice Hall, Inc., 1960), pp. 1039-40.
62. Massachusetts, New Jersey, Oklahoma, Pennsylvania, Rhode Island, and Vermont. *Ibid.*

Chapter III

The North Carolina Case: The 1957 Change

Introduction

The statutory changes made by the 1957 General Assembly of North Carolina with respect to the taxation of the net income of corporations were the most sweeping of any made since the state instituted the tax in 1921. In this and the following chapter the experience of North Carolina in connection with this revision is presented as a case study that is valuable in determining the effects of formula revisions and developing theories of income apportionment. The purpose of this chapter is to trace the developments leading to the change and to describe the revisions.

Apportionment Formulae Before 1957

GENERAL. The formula generally applicable to foreign corporations from 1921 to 1931 was a one-factor property formula; from 1931 to 1957 a two-factor property-manufacturing cost or property-sales formula was used, depending upon whether the corporation's business in the state was primarily manufacturing or selling. For other foreign corporations, not including public utilities, a one-factor gross receipts formula was prescribed.[1] Domestic corpora-

1. The gross receipts formula was applied to corporations "deriving profits principally from the holding or sale of intangible property" in 1921, to corporations "deriving profits principally from sources other than holding or sale of tangible property" in 1933, and to corporations having a principal business "other than that described in Subsection 1 [manu-

tions were taxed on their entire net income; but in arriving at net income they were permitted, subject to certain conditions and limitations, to deduct income taxed by other states.

PROPERTY FORMULA, 1921-1931. The one-factor formula, comprised of realty and tangible personalty, initially adopted by North Carolina was patterned after the one enacted in Connecticut in 1915. Several years of administrative practice and experience had been established under the Connecticut law, and the validity of the formula had been upheld by the Supreme Court.[2] A similar New York formula was upheld in 1924,[3] but in 1931 the Court held that the North Carolina formula, as applied to Hans Rees' Sons, Inc., "operated unreasonably and arbitrarily," reaching an unconstitutional result.[4]

TWO-FACTOR FORMULAE, 1931-1957. The 1931 General Assembly replaced the one-factor property formula with two two-factor formulae. For foreign corporations whose principal business in the state was manufacturing, the formula consisted of property and manufacturing cost; for those whose principal business was selling, property and sales. The property factor was the book value of realty and tangible personalty; manufacturing cost, "the total cost of manufacturing, collecting, assembling, or

facturing] or Subsection 2 [selling]" in 1941. *Public Laws of North Carolina* (1921), Chap. 34, Sec. 200; *ibid.* (1933), Chap. 445, Sec. 311; *ibid.* (1941), Chap. 50, Sec. 5.

2. *Underwood Typewriter Company* v. *Chamberlain*, 254 U.S. 113 (1920). For a detailed history of the development of formulae in North Carolina to 1953, see Eugene G. Shaw, *Comments on the Allocation Formulas for the Apportionment of Income and Franchise Taxes to the State of North Carolina* (General Assembly of North Carolina, Joint Finance Committee, 1953).

3. *Bass, Ratcliff & Gretton, Ltd.* v. *State Tax Comm'n*, 266 U.S. 271 (1924).

4. *Hans Rees' Sons, Inc.* v. *North Carolina*, 283 U.S. 123 (1931).

processing"; sales, "sales made through or by offices, agencies, or branches."[5]

These basic formulae remained substantially unchanged until 1957, but two amendments affecting income apportionment during the period should be noted. In 1943 the Commissioner of Revenue was authorized to add or substitute a payroll factor in the statutory formula in cases where it was determined that such a revised formula would more accurately reflect the income attributable to North Carolina.[6] Ten years later this relief provision was replaced by the establishment of the Tax Review Board, which was authorized to add or substitute the payroll factor, to permit separate accounting, or to allow some "other method of allocation." The burden rested on the taxpayer to show that the statutory formula was unreasonable, and the Board was to grant relief "only in cases of clear, cogent and convincing proof that the petitioning taxpayer is entitled thereto."[7]

The Problem

The over-all problem facing the state in the mid-fifties was that this state's tax structure, relative to those of other states, appeared to be unduly harsh on industry and thus was possibly a deterrent to economic development. A prime contributor to this forbidding appearance was the method of apportioning income of multi-state businesses. The formulae used certainly gave the impression that

5. *Public Laws of North Carolina* (1931), Chap. 427, Sec. 311.
6. *Ibid.* (1943), Chap. 400, Sec. 4.
7. *Session Laws of North Carolina* (1953), Chap. 1302, Sec. 4, Sec. 7. The Board was composed of the Commissioner of Revenue (Chairman), the Director of the Department of Tax Research, and the State Treasurer. In 1955 the Chairman of the Utilities Commission was added and the State Treasurer was made Chairman. The Commissioner of Revenue continued to serve in cases involving apportionment formulae under the franchise and income taxes, but in no other cases. (*Ibid.* [1955], Chap. 1350, Sec. 1.) See below, p. 37.

North Carolina was bent on extracting the constitutional maximum of taxes from multi-state businesses and was in some situations taxing income that could not be economically attributed to the state. This is seen in the separate treatment of domestic and foreign corporations, the statutory formulae applicable to foreign interstate corporations, and the statutory treatment of non-unitary income.

DOMESTIC V. FOREIGN CORPORATIONS. Domestic corporations were not allowed to apportion their income by formula. A domestic corporation doing business in other states could deduct out-of-state income if it was taxed by another state.[8] Thus a domestic corporation operating in states without corporate income taxes was taxed by North Carolina on all of its unitary income.

FORMULAE FOR FOREIGN CORPORATIONS. The formula used by a foreign corporation depended not on its principal business but its principal business in North Carolina. One principally manufacturing in the state used a property-manufacturing cost formula, while one principally selling in the state, though it be manufacturer, used a property-sales (through offices) formula. If a corporation had been manufacturing in another state that used similar formulae and selling through a North Carolina office, it would have been taxed on about 150 per cent of its income: roughly 100 per cent in the other state (property-

8. Before 1955 the definition of income taxed in another state was such that a domestic corporation could not deduct, with reference to income earned in a state allowing the deduction of federal income taxes, the amount of income represented by the federal income tax. In 1955 it was provided that income earned in another state be deemed taxed if any income tax was levied thereon, "regardless of any deductions, exemptions or credits allowed . . . in computing the tax." (*Ibid.* [1955], Chap. 1342.) The maximum deduction of income taxed in another state was the amount that would be attributed to the other state under the North Carolina formula provided for a foreign corporation (*Revenue Act*, Sec. 322 [10]).

manufacturing cost) and 50 per cent in North Carolina (property-sales). Of course, if both states had used a single uniform formula, regardless of the factors, the corporation would have been taxed on exactly 100 per cent of its income.

NON-UNITARY INCOME. The state provided that the entire net income of a foreign corporation be apportioned by formula, no separate allocation of non-unitary income (for example, rent from property not connected with the unitary business) being allowed. The administrator, however, on the grounds of constitutionality, did not include in apportionable income non-unitary income attributable to sources outside the state. Of course, non-unitary income attributable to sources within the state wound up being apportioned.

Developments Leading to Change

The above history and description of the apportionment formulae in use before 1957 show that the method of apportionment used by North Carolina had a forbidding appearance. In addition, the tax rate has been relatively high and no deduction of federal income taxes is allowed.[9] North Carolina gained the reputation of being a "high tax" state, and as the interstate operations of businesses increased there was mounting pressure for tax relief. Many legislators favored a change in this direction but for political reasons kept postponing any serious attempts to achieve it.

9. For an interstate comparison of the effective marginal state tax rates in 1955, taking into account the "reciprocal deductibility" of federal and state corporate income taxes, see *Report of the Governor's Minnesota Tax Study Committee* (1956), pp. 312-14. North Carolina ranked fourth among the 33 states, with its effective marginal rate being exceeded in only Mississippi, Massachusetts, and Wisconsin. Among the states ranked 1-17, only one allowed the deduction of federal taxes and one allowed a limited deduction; among those ranked 18-33, only one did not allow such deduction.

MINOR ADJUSTMENTS. The 1943 and 1953 amendments affecting income apportionment noted above enabled the Commissioner of Revenue, first, and later the Tax Review Board to grant tax relief in cases where the statutory formula was shown to be unreasonable. However, these minor adjustments did not stem the tide of discontent: some of the state's manufacturers, especially those in the major industries of tobacco and textiles, voiced dissatisfaction at the absence of a sales factor, and those with domestic charters pleaded for equal treatment with foreign corporations, that is, apportionment by formula. Both the Commissioner and the Board handled only extreme "hardship" cases where there was a question of whether the law would stand up in court. Though the Board was empowered to allow some "other method of allocation," it was very reluctant to allow the sales factor, since the legislature had not seen fit to include it in the statutory formula (for manufacturers). At the same time, the limited granting of a sales factor to foreign corporations increased the discontent of domestic multi-state corporations, some of which threatened to domesticate in other states so that they could petition the Tax Review Board for equal treatment.

TAX STUDY COMMISSION: RECOMMENDATIONS. Other approaches having failed to solve the problem and with mounting pressure for a change in the statutory formulae, the legislature, in the closing days of the 1955 session, passed a resolution authorizing the Governor to appoint a commission to study and make recommendations for revising the Revenue Act.[10] The resolution called for a

10. The resolution labeled the body as the Commission for the Study of the Revenue Structure of the State, but it soon became known as the Tax Study Commission. (Resolution 49, *Session Laws of North Carolina* [1955], pp. 1710-12.) The resolution was reported out of committee in the House on May 12, passed the House May 17, reported

study of the whole revenue system, but there is no doubt
as to the principal objective: a study of the apportionment
formulae.[11]   To make a thorough study of the economic
impact of state and local taxes in North Carolina and other
southeastern states, an economist from another part of
the country was hired by the Commission.[12]   To analyze
and appraise the economic condition, characteristics, and
potential of the state, economists and sociologists of the
state's University system were called upon by the Commission.[13]   Responding to the general invitation of the Com-

---

out of committee in the Senate May 19, passed the Senate May 20, and
was enrolled May 21.

11. The Commission was directed to (1) recommend changes that
"would provide a more easily understandable and workable system of
revenue laws," (2) recommend changes "to the end that our revenue
system may be stable and equitable, and yet so fair when compared with
the tax structures of other states, that business enterprises and persons
would be encouraged . . . to move . . . into the State," (3) "make a
report upon the economic impact of the North Carolina tax structure
upon the business enterprises of various types of industry, as compared
with those of other southeastern states," (4) "make recommendations
for long range revenue planning," and (5) "make a study of allocation
formulas . . . , together with recommendations as to flexible adjustment
procedures which may be provided, in cases of inequity of application
of . . . formulas."

12. The five-hundred-page study by Leslie E. Carbert was completed in October, 1956, and published by the Commission under the
title *The Impact of State and Local Taxes in North Carolina and the
Southeastern States.*

13. Papers presented at April, 1956, conferences: Gordon W. Black-
well, "The Problem of Objectives and Factors in the Development of
North Carolina"; Daniel O. Price, "Population Trends and Migration";
George L. Simpson, Jr., "Trends in the Occupational Structure"; Milton
S. Heath, "Some Basic Trends in American and Southern Industrializa-
tion"; Lowell D. Ashby, "Per Capita Personal Income Growth Since
1939"; Paul Guthrie, "The Wage Structure"; Harriet L. Herring, "The
Industrial Situation in North Carolina"; G. S. Logsdon, "Some Factors
in Industrialization"; George L. Simpson, Jr., "Higher Education and
Economic Advance." *Studies of Per Capita Income in North Carolina,*
A Report by an Interinstitutional Committee of North Carolina State
College and University of North Carolina at Chapel Hill, March, 1956,
contained the following: Lowell D. Ashby and W. Allen Spivey, "Per
Capita Income Payments to Individuals, Their Nature and Reliability";
Charles E. Bishop, "The Income of North Carolina Farm People";
Harriet L. Herring, "Factors in North Carolina's Manufacturing Industry

mission, various individuals, businesses, trade associations, and professional groups presented written briefs to and participated in oral discussions before the Commission.[14] Working very closely with the Commission was the Department of Tax Research, which was directed to study the topics of corporate and individual income taxes, the impact of taxation on industry, and allocation formulae "with major emphasis upon corporate taxation."[15]

After receiving study results and many suggestions and complaints,[16] the Income Tax Committee reported to

Contributing to Low Rank in Per Capita Income"; Herbert A. Aurback and C. Horace Hamilton, "Comparison of North Carolina with the United States, the South and Other States on Selected Socio-Economic Variables"; Herbert A. Aurback and C. Horace Hamilton, "The Relationship of Income Measures to Population Factors and to Other Measures of Economic and Social Well-Being"; Staff of the Department of Agricultural Economics of North Carolina State College and W. E. Hendrix, "The Problem of Low Incomes in North Carolina's Nonfarm Economy." For a summary of the findings, see *Report of the Tax Study Commission of the State of North Carolina* (Raleigh, 1956), pp. 3-4.

14. The briefs, in outline form, were mimeographed. The typewritten minutes of the Commission are filed in the offices of the Department of Tax Research, Raleigh.

15. *Minutes of the Tax Study Commission,* meeting of July 28, 1955. The Department's studies included *Historical Background of the North Carolina Income Tax* (Raleigh, N.C.: Department of Tax Research, January 5, 1956; mimeographed); *The Allocation of Net Income of Corporations Engaged in Interstate Business* (Raleigh, N.C.: Department of Tax Research; January 16, 1956; mimeographed); *Corporation Income Taxes: Consolidated Returns of Affiliated Corporations* (Raleigh, N.C.: Staff of Commission and Department of Tax Research; February 7, 1956; mimeographed).

16. One conclusion of the economist making the impact study was that, contrary to the general belief, it appeared that North Carolina, relative to other southeastern states, did not compensate for high income taxes with low property taxes (*Minutes of the Tax Study Commission,* meeting of June 19, 1956); the Commissioner of Revenue proposed that domestic and foreign corporations engaged in interstate business be permitted to use the same apportionment formula (*ibid.,* meeting of July 18, 1956); the Director of the Department of Conservation and Development, representatives of Chambers of Commerce, and businessmen contended that the state's tax structure was a deterrent to industrial expansion (*ibid.,* meetings of August 16 and September 11, 1956).

the full Commission,[17] which incorporated into its *Report* practically verbatim the Committee's recommendations and arguments concerning income apportionment. The Commission recommended (1) that domestic and foreign corporations be taxed according to the same rules and only on income reasonably attributed to North Carolina; (2) that income from investment property (non-unitary income) be separately allocated; (3) that net apportionable income (unitary income) be apportioned by formula, manufacturing and selling firms using property-payroll-sales and others (not including utilities[18]) using gross receipts.[19]

In the Commission's words, it had "formulated a plan for the allocation or apportionment of net income with the purpose of providing for the equitable taxation of net income as between competing corporations and of

17. *A Partial Report of the Income Tax Committee to the Commission for the Study of the Revenue Structure of the State* (*Minutes of the Tax Study Commission,* meeting of August 16, 1956; mimeographed); *A Supplementary Report of the Income Tax Committee to the Commission for the Study of the Revenue Structure of the State* (*Minutes of the Tax Study Commission,* meeting of September 11, 1956; mimeographed). With its final report on September 12, 1956, the Committee was dissolved.

18. Special formulae were recommended for public utilities, which are not included in this study. Factors in these formulae were: for railroads, railway operating revenue; for telephone companies, gross operating revenue; for motor carriers of passengers, vehicle miles and gross operating revenue. In 1956 the statutes did not provide for apportionment of the net income of public utilities, but rather the apportionment of gross operating revenue from which a proportional part of operating expenses were deductible. The recommendations of the Commission were enacted into law (*General Statutes of North Carolina.* Sec. 105-134).

19. Gross receipts were not to include the gross receipts from sources the net income from which was to be separately allocated.

It was recommended that these apportionment rules apply to multi-state unincorporated businesses owned by a non-resident individual or by a partnership having any non-resident members. In 1956 the statutes contained no provision for apportioning interstate income of unincorporated businesses; the recommendation was enacted into law (*ibid.,* Sec. 105-142).

providing a method of allocation which would encourage, or, at worst, would not discourage, industrial development in the State."[20]   It believed that with the formulae recommended (1) the state would not tax more of the income of corporations than was reasonably attributable to the state, (2) the state would be placed "in a more competitive position among her sister states in this respect," (3) the state would not tax corporations having regional distribution offices located therein on income from sales made throughout the region, and (4) corporations would not be encouraged to move offices to other states to reduce their income taxes.   The Commission asserted (5) that it was not its intention "to incorporate a general tax reduction to all corporations into the allocation formula as it is believed that this is a question of rate adjustment and not one of determination of the proper tax base."[21]

The Commission's recommendation to treat domestic and foreign corporations alike was designed to put them on an equal footing.   It could find no justification, other than a legalistic one, for taxing domestic corporations on income attributable to other states while foreign corporations with which they were competing were not so taxed. The recommendation of separate allocation of non-

20. *Report of the Tax Study Commission,* p. 29.
21. *Ibid.* The Department of Tax Research, in making suggestions to the Income Tax Committee, understood that the Committee had six specific objectives: the five stipulated here plus "a net reduction of the income tax base of interstate manufacturers as a group."   With six listed, the last one stipulated here read: "but to write no general tax reduction to all corporations or to all manufacturing corporations into. . . ."   See *Suggested Statute for Allocation of the Net Income of Corporations to North Carolina for Income Tax Purposes and of Capital Stock for Franchise Tax Purposes* (Raleigh, N.C.: Department of Tax Research, July 16, 1956; mimeographed), and *Suggested Provisions for Allocation of Income of Interstate Corporations Submitted to the Income Tax Committee of the Tax Study Commission by the Department of Tax Research* (Raleigh, N.C.: Department of Tax Research, July 17, 1956; mimeographed).

unitary income brought the statutes into conformity with constitutional law and the administrative practice of the Commissioner of Revenue.

In recommending the application of the same apportionment formula to all manufacturing and selling corporations, the Commission argued that applying different formulae according to the principal business within the state "almost inevitably" resulted in many firms' being taxed on more income than was reasonably attributable to the state. In justifying its recommendation of the three-factor property-payroll-sales formula, the Commission asserted that "Property, representing capital, is, of course, a primary income producer," that "the utilization of labor is believed to be an income producing function," and that it is "believed that selling is an income producing function . . . regardless of whether the property is manufactured in this State by the seller or not." Regarding the sales factor, the Commission accepted the following argument: "In the final analysis, all property which is manufactured is manufactured for the purpose of eventual sale for profit. Without the sale there can be no profit."

The property factor recommended by the Commission was the same as that in the existing law except that the capitalized value of rented property was to be included. This change was considered desirable in light of the increased renting of industrial property. The value of property yielding non-unitary income, which was separately allocated, was not to be included.

The recommended payroll factor included compensation of regularly employed personnel, excluding executive officers, the amounts attributed to the state of principal activity of the employee. Executive salaries were excluded because of the frequent difficulty of determining the state of principal activity and because their inclusion might induce companies to base executives outside the state. An employee's salary was to be attributed to the state in which he spent the largest number of working days, rather than prorated, because of less difficulty in compliance and administration and the belief that errors would largely compensate each other.[22]

The Commission recommended that the sales factor attribute sales to the state of destination of shipments. The destination basis was chosen by the Commission on the grounds that (1) it reflects income earned from sales activity more accurately than any other basis, (2) it is more easily complied with and administered than others, (3) it is subject to less "control" for tax avoidance purposes than the through-offices basis, and (4) it would not discourage the establishment of regional sales offices within the state. The Commission did not explicitly list, as a reason for choosing the destination basis, the tax relief that would accrue to North Carolina manufacturers selling nationally, but in the paragraph assessing the effects it did state: "Adoption of this definition . . . would be beneficial to corporations with sales from North Carolina offices or distribution points to customers outside of this State."[23]

To prevent tax avoidance in certain cases under the apportionment method recommended, the Commission proposed that a corporation must be doing business in at least one other state to apportion its income. Corporations doing business exclusively in North Carolina would pay on their entire net income. This was designed to prevent a 100 per cent North Carolina corporation (one having no business operations or property outside the

22. The payroll factor that the Tax Review Board was permitted to authorize attributed salaries of North Carolina residents to North Carolina regardless of the location of activity. (*Session Laws of North Carolina* [1953], Chap. 1302.)

23. *Report of the Tax Study Commission*, p. 33. See above, n. 21.

state) from apportioning income to a state that does not have jurisdiction to tax the corporation—for example, apportioning on the basis of mail order shipments to another state.[24]

TAX STUDY COMMISSION: REACTIONS. The Commission began work in the summer of 1955, the report was issued in November, 1956, and the General Assembly convened in January, 1957. Until the last date, practically no criticism of the proposed change in business taxation was voiced. Considerable effort was expended, especially by the Governor and the Commission Chairman, in publicizing the work of the Commission and "selling" the people on the need for revamping the tax laws. Various changes affecting individuals were pointed to, but major attention was given to the change in the apportionment of business income, the theme of the numerous speeches being that the formula revision was needed to stimulate industrial development.[25] Generally speaking, the editors of the state's newspapers, having argued the need for tax revision while the Commission was at work,[26] endorsed its

24. The proposed statute provided: "The entire business of a corporation shall be deemed to have been transacted and conducted within this State if such corporation is not subject to a net income tax or a franchise tax measured by net income in any other state . . . or any foreign country, or would not be subject to a net income tax in any other such taxing jurisdiction if such other taxing jurisdiction adopted the net income tax laws of this State."

25. For newspaper accounts of some of the speeches, see *Charlotte Observer*, July 3, 1956; *Raleigh News and Observer*, August 12, September 15, 1956; *Durham Herald*, September 2, 1956; *Greensboro Daily News*, September 23, 1956. For the Governor's defense of the change as presented to the General Assembly in his Biennial Message, see *Senate Journal*, 1957, pp. 62-64. Copies of many of the speeches are in the files of the Department of Tax Research, Raleigh. For a very colorful depiction of the situation, see "The North Carolina of 1956," *The State*, XXIV (December 29, 1956), pp. 7, 39.

26. For example, *Roanoke Rapids Herald*, January 22, 1956; *Asheville Citizen*, March 30, May 24, June 23, 1956; *Shelby Star*, March 31, 1956; *Greensboro Daily News*, April 24, May 22, July 10, 1956; *Durham Herald*, May 22, 28, 1956; *Sanford Herald*, May 25, 1956; *Winston-*

recommendations.[27]   However, there were some expressions of caution: the need for careful study and listening to both sides by legislators and the public; the fear of a broadened sales tax base to offset the revenue loss; and the importance of maintaining or improving the level of state services, particularly education.[28]

There was very little opposition to the proposed tax revision.   The principal criticism of opponents, both in and out of the legislature, was that the revised formula granted tax relief to business at the expense of public services, particularly education.   Proponents argued that a long-run compatibility between tax revision and increased support of public schools existed.[29]   It should be observed that the apathy of the general public was disturbed hardly any by the issue.   Moreover, many legis-

---

Salem Sentinel, July 2, 1956; *Winston-Salem Journal,* July 7, 1956; *Wilmington Star News,* September 17, 1956.

27. For example, *Gastonia Gazette,* November 30, 1956; *Hickory Record,* November 30, 1956; *Asheville Times,* December 1, 1956; *Charlotte News,* December 1, 1956; *Durham Herald,* December 1, 1956; *Raleigh Times,* December 1, 1956; *Wilmington Star News,* December 1, 1956; *Greeensboro Daily News,* December 2, 1956; *Rocky Mount Telegram,* December 2, 1956; *Durham Sun,* December 3, 1956; *Sanford Herald,* December 3, 1956; *Morganton News-Herald,* December 6, 1956.

28. *High Point Enterprise,* August 12, November 30, 1956; *Kings Mountain Herald,* October 18, 1956; *Raleigh News and Observer,* November 30, December 1, 1956, February 28, April 23, 1957; *Concord Tribune,* December 6, 1956.   The *News and Observer* laid down this rule: "All of the recommendations are designed to remove inequities in the present tax laws.   If the Legislature finds that any recommendation removes a real inequity, without creating the necessity for a greater inequity in the form of other taxes, the recommendation should be adopted.   Recommendations which do not meet that standard should be rejected."

29. For criticisms made by particular persons and organizations and rejoinders, see *Durham Herald,* January 21, 1957; *Raleigh News and Observer,* February 20, April 19, 22, 23, 24, May 18, 23, 28, 1957; *Greensboro Daily News,* February 20, 1957; *Raleigh Times,* February 21, April 22, 1957; *Asheville Citizen,* February 24, 28, 1957; *Winston-Salem Journal,* February 27, 1957; *Charlotte Observer,* April 28, 1957; *House Journal,* 1957, pp. 1121-23; *Senate Journal,* 1957, pp. 507-8.

lators were frank in saying, regarding the briefings on the apportionment formula, that they did not know "what it was all about."[30]   And finally, the legislators were placed in a rather vulnerable position in voting, inasmuch as state officials were in essence advising the business world that if the tax law were not changed North Carolina would be, as far as the tax factor is concerned, a relatively poor business location.[31]

Voting down efforts to postpone the effective date of the new formula, the two houses of the legislature passed the revenue bill by overwhelming majorities.[32]   Several factors may help account for such a resounding adoption. One was the tremendous popular support enjoyed by the Governor, Luther H. Hodges.   A major part of his program was the revamping of the tax laws: this had been well publicized and was accepted by the public with very little questioning.   Another was the stature of the Commission: the members were men of prestige representing different economic interests and geographical areas in the state.   Still another factor was the increased propensity of the legislature to amend the tax law.   After the major changes of the early thirties, a period of about two decades ensued in which tax law amendments were few.   Since 1953 amendments have been frequent and significant.   Among the reasons for this shift on the part of the legislature are the following: (1) prior to the fifties the huge budget surpluses were never expected officially, which tended to make amendment of the laws more diffi-

30. *Raleigh News and Observer*, February 27, 28, 1957. See Institute of Government Legislative Service, *Weekly Legislative Summary*, June 1, 1957.
31. See *Raleigh News and Observer*, May 21, 1957.
32. The count was 95-8 in the House, *House Journal*, 1957, p. 1121; 44-2 in the Senate, *Senate Journal*, 1957, pp. 755-56. See *Charlotte Observer*, May 29, 30, June 5, 6, 8, 10, 1957. The last reference is to an editorial: "Corporate Tax Reduction: A Risk Worth the Taking."

cult; (2) the pressure prior to the fifties was directed more towards lowering the tax rate than toward changing the apportionment formula, the former engendering more opposition than the latter; (3) even business representatives in the legislature were reluctant to change the law, one reason being that the high federal corporate and excess profits taxes caused the federal government, in effect, to "pay" a large percentage of the state corporate income tax and another reason being the fear that a reduction in corporate taxes would open the door to a reduction in the sales tax;[33] and (4) there appears to have been an increased willingness on the part of the legislature to adopt recommendations growing out of studies. An additional factor is embodied in the observations dealing with the legislators in the preceding paragraph: the legislators were maneuvered into the position of voting for or against industrial development.

The Change

Except for a few minor changes, the law enacted was identical to the proposed statutory provisions presented by the Commission in the appendix to its *Report*.[34] The recommendations of the Commission, as presented earlier in this chapter, were enacted into law.

Beginning July 1, 1957, corporate income was taxed under the new law. Non-unitary income (less related expenses) is separately allocated: interest, dividends, and royalties from intangible property to the state in which the

33. They reasoned that this was very likely in light of the war-time budget surpluses and the strong sentiment against the sales tax, which had been adopted in the depression as an emergency measure, had been one of the major issues in two subsequent gubernatorial campaigns, and was attacked by lobbyists as the "poor man's tax." They reasoned that later, in the post-war period with the increased revenue needs, the corporate tax, rather than the sales tax, would more likely be increased.
34. Pp. 105-7.

principal place of business of the corporation is located, and rents and royalties from tangible property to the state in which the property is located. Capital gains and losses are allocated on the basis of the principal place of business in the case of corporate stocks and location in the case of tangible property. The allocation of non-unitary income from any other investments is according to the business situs of the investment; if the situs is partly within and partly without North Carolina, the income is apportioned as is unitary income.

The non-unitary net income having been directly allocated, the remainder of the net income, or unitary net income, of manufacturing and selling firms is apportioned on the basis of the three-factor property-payroll-sales formula described above.

All corporations, domestic or foreign, doing business in at least one other state apportion their income. Those doing business in no other state are taxed by North Carolina on the entire net income.[35]

With the institution of the foregoing procedure, the authority of the Tax Review Board had to be revised. With the payroll factor in the statutory formula, the Board was authorized to permit separate accounting or allow some "other method of allocation" if it determines that one of these more accurately reflects income attributable to the state than does the statutory formula.[36]

Conclusion

North Carolina's pre-1957 tax structure, because of the method of apportioning income, was relatively harsh on multi-state business. Growing demands for a change in the apportionment formula were not satisfied by several

35. See above, pp. 43-44, and n. 24.
36. Before, it was authorized also to add or substitute the payroll factor. See above, p. 34.

minor relief provisions, so a Tax Study Commission was established for the primary purpose of studying the apportionment formula. This resulted in recommendations for the most sweeping changes ever made in North Carolina corporate income taxation, and these were enacted into law with little difficulty. In fact, the formula revision seems to have helped carry through the legislature the numerous minor changes in other taxes recommended by the Commission. At the same time, the existence of these minor changes demonstrated that the 1957 operation was, to some extent at least, a general revamping of the tax laws.

Chapter IV

The North Carolina Case:
Effects of Change

Introduction

In making its recommendations, the Tax Study Commission estimated the effects of the changes on state tax revenue. Also, in presenting the case for the change in the apportionment method, it expressed its expectations or hopes regarding the effect on industrial development. The purpose of this chapter is to present the actual effects of the formula revision, insofar as they can be determined, and to compare them with the expected effect on revenue and industrial development. The effects of this change should be relevant to all states taxing corporate net income.

Expected Effects

REVENUE. The Commission estimated that the enactment of its recommended apportionment method would result in a loss of revenue of approximately $7 million for the fiscal year 1957-1958.[1] It was estimated that corporate income tax collections would be $45.6 million in the

1. *Report of the Tax Study Commission of the State of North Carolina* (Raleigh, 1956), p. 30. More exactly, it was estimated that $6.87 million less would be collected under the corporate income tax, $.35 million less under the corporate franchise tax, and $.15 million more under the individual income tax. (From worksheets in the Department of Tax Research.) Corporations use the same apportionment formula under the franchise tax as under the income tax. Dividends are taxable to individuals to the extent that the corporation's income is not taxable by North Carolina.

fiscal year 1957-1958 if the formula were not changed, and $38.7 million if it were, or 15.1 per cent less. Though the great majority of corporate taxpayers was expected to experience a decrease or no change in tax liability, a few were expected to have an increase.[2]

To estimate the revenue loss, the Department of Tax Research estimated the reduction that would have occurred in 1954 tax liabilities under the proposed formula and increased this by the percentage that tax collections were expected to increase between the fiscal years 1954-1955 and 1957-1958. This gave the $6.9 million reduction in 1957 corporate income tax liabilities.[3] In making the estimate for 1954, corporations were separated into two groups: (1) those filing under Tax Review Board orders, and (2) those filing under the statutory formula. The task with respect to the few dozen corporations in group (1) was to determine the additional reduction afforded by the three-factor formula, for they were already enjoying some reduction of varying degrees. For all others, the task was to determine the difference in revenue if they had been allowed to file under the proposed statutory formula instead of the one in effect. Analyzing every one of the corporations in group (1), as opposed to including them in the population from which a sample was drawn, was advantageous because data filed with the Tax Review Board were available, and these firms accounted for a substantial portion of the corporate income tax collections.

In the case of group (1) corporations, property data were used with no adjustment for rental property. Where payroll data were not available, manufacturing cost data

2. *Report*, p. 30.
3. $6.8 million reduction for manufacturing and trade corporations. The 1954 reduction for domestic manufacturing and trade corporations was $2,018,000; for foreign, $3,043,000; increased by 32.2 per cent and 35.8 per cent, respectively, the estimated 1957 reductions were $2,668,000 and $4,133,000, respectively.

Table IV

ESTIMATED AND ACTUAL REDUCTIONS IN NORTH CAROLINA
INCOME TAX LIABILITIES, BY TYPE OF BUSINESS AND
TYPE OF CORPORATION, 1957
(Thousands of dollars)

Type of business	ESTIMATED REDUCTION			ACTUAL REDUCTION		
	Total	Domestic	Foreign	Total	Domestic	Foreign
Manufacturing[a]						
Food and feed....	225	156	69	68	35	33
Forest products..	1,108	566	542	372	48	324
Mineral, chemical, metal.........	168	74	94	4	*	4
Textile..........	2,082	1,663	419	789	837	(49)
Tobacco.........	2,225	83	2,143	1,899	3	1,896
Other..........	567	17	550	433	65	368
Total mfg......	6,375	2,558	3,817	3,565	987	2,577
Trade[b]						
Automotive......	123	1	122	(428)	(*)	(428)
Beverage, food, drug.........	53	24	29	(31)	1	(32)
Equipment and supplies.......	167	43	124	105	2	102
General merchandise.......	36	—	36	42	2	40
Unclassified......	47	42	5	(8)	(1)	(6)
Total trade....	425	110	316	(319)	5	(324)
Total manufacturing and trade........	6,801	2,668	4,133	3,245	992	2,253
Other[c]...........	71	71	—	124	147	(23)
Grand total........	6,872	2,739	4,133	3,369	1,139	2,230

Source: Adapted from worksheets of the North Carolina Department of Tax Research, Raleigh.
Figures in parentheses represent increases.
* Less than $500.
a Includes only those actually manufacturing in North Carolina.
b Includes out-of-state manufacturers selling in North Carolina.
c Includes agriculture, construction, finance, public utility, recreation, and service, as shown in the Appendix. See n. 14 below.

were used for manufacturing corporations and estimates
from a sample for selling corporations. Where sales data
were not available, estimates were used.

In the case of group (2) corporations, a sample was

used. This sample consisted of usable questionnaires completed for the Carbert study. The questionnaire requested data on property, including rental property, and payrolls, but not destination sales data.[4]

The estimated reduction in revenue, by type of business, is shown in Table IV.

INDUSTRIAL DEVELOPMENT. In its *Report* the Commission was somewhat more restrained in its estimates of the effect of the revision on industrial development than were some of the members and the Governor in their statements. The Commission's words: "It is hoped that removal of excessive harshness in the existing formulae will eliminate a deterrent to further industrialization which will accelerate economic activity in the State with an eventual recoupment of immediate tax losses."[5]

The state, in its advertising for industry after the change, gave the change top billing. In a November, 1957, advertisement headed "North Carolina Reduces Taxes" a member of the Board of Conservation and Development announced that taxes on companies having interstate operations had been reduced "to encourage more industry to locate and expand in the state" and that already two major industrial plants would be built as a result of the change.[6] A couple of years later it was stated in the advertising that the 1957 revision did not reduce revenue as much as expected "because more and more industries have been attracted into this favorable business climate."[7]

4. See Leslie E. Carbert, *The Impact of State and Local Taxes in North Carolina and the Southeastern States* (North Carolina Commission for the Study of the Revenue Structure of the State, 1956), pp. 363-67, for reproduction of questionnaire.

5. *Report*, p. 30.

6. *New York Times*, November 17, 1957, sec. 10. The two plants were identified: Allied-Kennecott Titanium Corporation at Wilmington; R. J. Reynolds Tobacco Company in Winston-Salem area.

7. See inside back cover, *North Carolina State and Local Taxes,*

The Actual Effects: Revenue

TAX LIABILITIES, ALL CORPORATIONS, 1957. Since the effective date of the new formula was July 1, 1957, the year 1957 was a "split formula" year, taxpayers applying the old formula to the period prior to July 1, 1957, and the new formula to the period subsequent to June 30, 1957. By applying each formula in turn to the 1957 incomes of the taxpayers, the effect of the formula revision on revenue is determined with a minimum of interference from extraneous factors.[8] The difference between tax liabilities that would have existed had the old formulae been in effect all year and those that would have existed had the new been in effect all year are shown in Table IV above. Compared with the estimated losses of $6.9 million for all corporations and $6.8 million for manufacturing and selling corporations, the losses were $3.4 million and $3.2 million, respectively, or about half that expected.

Corporate tax collections for the fiscal year 1957-1958 amounted to $43.5 million.[9] If the old method had remained in effect throughout 1957, this amount would have been about $45.2 million; had the new applied throughout, about $41.8 million, or 7.5 per cent less than under the old. The $45.2 million is very close to the earlier estimate of $45.6 million, especially in light of the 1957-1958 recession.

Several factors may help account for the actual revenue loss being only half the estimated. First, the sample used for the group (2) corporations referred to above was very small and not truly random. The estimate was most

Effective July 1, 1959, published by the North Carolina Department of Conservation and Development.

8. Actually each taxpayer made these calculations in the return, prorating the apportioned amounts on the basis of the number of days in the income year before July 1 and the number after June 30.

9. North Carolina, *Statistics of Taxation* (1960), p. 97.

accurate for tobacco manufacturers (Table IV), who were generally in group (1). Second, the sales factor, which had to be estimated for most corporations in both groups, was generally underestimated. This affected especially out-of-state manufacturers selling in North Carolina (note automotive group in Table IV).[10] Third, the recession caused the actual reduction to be less than it would have been: with higher profits the absolute difference in tax liabilities under the two would have been greater. Fourth, the method used to estimate the loss probably overstated the loss attributable to the direct allocation of income.[11] Finally, the Commission appears to have exercised caution in estimating the reduction—an underestimate of the loss might have created a very unpleasant situation politically.

While the formula revision had the effect of reducing total corporate income tax revenue by 7.5 per cent, it affected the tax liabilities of only about 6 per cent of the corporations filing returns. This is due to the following facts: less than two-thirds of those filing reported taxable income, most of these did not engage in multi-state business, and some remained under Tax Review Board orders. The number affected and the amounts of change in their tax liabilities (assuming the law had been in effect all year) are shown in Table V. On the basis of both the

10. For one large firm, which has a small portion of its manufacturing facilities in North Carolina, the underestimate of the sales factor alone would account for over $.5 million of the difference between the estimated and actual reductions.

11. The loss for 1954 included the effect of allocating non-unitary income directly (as well as use of the three-factor formula by both domestic and foreign corporations). This total for 1954 was expanded by the expected percentage increase in tax collections between the years 1954-55 and 1957-58. Since non-unitary income is probably more stable than unitary income, the loss due to direct allocation in 1954 should have been increased by a lower percentage than the loss due to use of the three-factor formula. (Three-fourths of the corporations participating in this study reported non-unitary income to be more stable than unitary income between 1958 and 1959.)

Table V

NUMBER OF CORPORATIONS AND AMOUNT OF CHANGE IN
TAX LIABILITIES, BY TYPE OF BUSINESS AND
TYPE OF CORPORATION, 1957
(Amounts in thousands)

Type of corporation	NUMBER OF CORPORATIONS AND AMOUNT OF CHANGE				
	Total	Total mfg. & trade	Mfg.	Trade	Other
All corporations					
Number receiving increases.	368	312	60	252	56
Amount of increase........	$1,259	$1,221	$ 532	$ 689	$ 39
Number receiving decreases	629	548	162	386	81
Amount of decrease.......	$4,628	$4,466	$4,097	$ 369	$162
Number affected..........	997	860	222	638	137
Net decrease (increase)....	$3,369	$3,245	$3,565	$(319)	$124
Domestic corporations					
Number receiving increases.	47	25	8	17	22
Amount of increase........	$ 16	$ 13	$ 9	$ 3	$ 4
Number receiving decreases	118	75	44	31	43
Amount of decrease.......	$1,155	$1,004	$ 996	$ 8	$151
Number affected..........	165	100	52	48	65
Net decrease (increase)....	$1,139	$ 992	$ 987	$ 5	$147
Foreign corporations					
Number receiving increases.	321	287	52	235	34
Amount of increase........	$1,243	$1,208	$ 523	$ 685	$ 35
Number receiving decreases	511	473	118	355	38
Amount of decrease.......	$3,474	$3,462	$3,100	$ 361	$ 12
Number affected..........	832	760	170	590	72
Net decrease (increase)....	$2,230	$2,253	$2,577	$(324)	$(23)

Source: Worksheets of the North Carolina Department of Tax Research, Raleigh. For detailed breakdown see the Appendix.

proportion of affected firms receiving decreases and the
amount of decrease relative to the amount of increase, the
domestic corporations, as opposed to the foreign, and the
manufacturing corporations, as opposed to the trade or

selling, were treated more favorably by the revision. Whereas 75 per cent of the affected domestic manufacturing and selling corporations received decreases that, in the aggregate, were offset by increases to the extent of only 1.3 per cent, 62 per cent of the foreign received decreases that were offset 35 per cent. However, related to total tax liabilities, the net decrease was greater for foreign manufacturing and selling firms than for domestic.[12] Primarily responsible for this is the fact that practically all of the $1.9 million net decrease for tobacco manufacturers accrued to foreign corporations. On all three bases the manufacturing corporations are shown to have fared better than the selling corporations. Whereas 73 per cent of the affected manufacturing firms received decreases, the aggregate of which was offset 13 per cent by increases, 60 per cent of the selling firms received decreases that were more than offset by increases nearly twice as large in amount. As groups, then, selling firms experienced an increase in tax liabilities, while manufacturing firms experienced a decrease.[13] The experience of firms in different industry groups varied, as indicated by the detailed data presented in the Appendix. For the 860 manufacturing and selling corporations[14] affected by

12. Relative to 1957 income tax liabilities of $13.7 million and $19.1 million for domestic and foreign (*Statistics of Taxation* [1960], pp. 104-5), respectively, the net decreases were 7.3 per cent and 11.9 per cent. (Since these tax liabilities are those actually incurred, not those that would have been incurred had the formula not been revised, and since these data are liabilities and not fiscal year collections, the absolute percentages are not comparable with the 7.5 per cent referred to for all corporations.)

13. Relative to 1957 income tax liabilities of $25.2 million and $7.6 million for manufacturing and selling corporations (*ibid.*, p. 102), respectively, the reduction was 14.2 per cent and the increase 4.2 per cent.

14. Also shown in the Appendix are data for corporations other than those included in this study. Some construction companies are classified as manufacturing by the Department of Revenue, and some small trucking firms (here classified as public utilities) were affected.

Table VI

APPORTIONMENT PERCENTAGES OF 123 CORPORATIONS, NEW LAW RELATIVE TO OLD LAW, BY TYPE OF CORPORATION AND TYPE OF BUSINESS, 1957, 1958, AND 1959

Year	All						Domestic						Foreign					
	Manufacturing			Selling			Manufacturing			Selling			Manufacturing			Selling		
	Incr.	Decr.	Unch.	Incr.	Decr.	Unch.	Incr.	Decr.	Unch.	Incr.	Decr.	Unch.	Incr.	Decr.	Unch.	Incr.	Decr.	Unch.
1957a........	9	37	10	27	35	3	0	9	8	3	4	0	9	28	2	24	31	3
1958........	13	36	9	27	35	3	0	11	7	3	4	0	13	25	2	24	31	3
1959........	12	37	9	27	35	3	0	11	7	3	4	0	12	26	2	24	31	3

Source: Data obtained from individual corporations by interview and questionnaire. The 1957 data are apportionment percentages actually used in the returns for this "split formula" year. The 1958 and 1959 data are the percentages used compared with those that would have been used had the law not been changed. For domestic corporations not filing under Tax Review Board orders, the percentage under the old law is more accurately referred to as the percentage of income taxable in North Carolina. Corporations filing under administrative orders of the Tax Review Board and remaining thereunder after June 30, 1957, are classified under "unchanged" (see Table VII).

a One domestic manufacturing firm was using separate accounting before July 1, 1957; one foreign manufacturing firm was not subject to the North Carolina income tax in 1957.

the new law, nearly two-thirds had decreased liabilities aggregating $4.5 million and over a third increased liabilities aggregating $1.2 million.

Since information from the individual returns of these corporations was not available, as explained in Chapter I, the effect of the revision on the individual corporate tax liabilities for the population could not be ascertained. However, such data were obtained by interview and questionnaire for a sample.

EFFECT ON SAMPLE CORPORATIONS, 1957, 1958, 1959. From 126 sample corporations, data were obtained for 1957, 1958, and 1959, as described in Chapter I. Since the 1957 sample data duplicate to some extent the population data, a check on the reliability of the sample is provided. Included in the sample is at least one-ninth of the firms that experienced changes in 1957 tax liabilities because of the formula revision.[15] The sample corporations appear to be representative of the population of corporations affected by the revision, but the tax data supplied by the sample corporations show some bias owing to the reluctance of those receiving substantial tax relief to divulge tax data.[16]

15. Of the 126 participating firms, 109 made alternative tax computations for the author, 96, or 11.2 per cent of the 860, showing different 1957 tax liabilities under the old and new formulae.

16. Of 860 manufacturing and selling corporations experiencing a change in tax liabilities, 548, or 63.7 per cent, experienced decreases; of 108 sample corporations experiencing a change in apportionment percentages, 72, or 66.7 per cent, experienced decreases. Similar percentages, for population and sample respectively, are: for manufacturing corporations, 73.0 and 80.4; for selling or trade corporations, 60.5 and 56.5; for domestic corporations, 75.0 and 81.2; for foreign corporations, 62.2 and 64.1. (Cf. Tables V and VI.) For the purpose of checking the reliability of the sample, a better comparison is that between the sample corporations experiencing a change in tax liabilities and the population. Of 96 such sample corporations, 61, or 63.5 per cent, experienced decreases, compared with 63.7 per cent for the population. Population and sample percentages for manufacturing corpora-

The effect of the new formula on the apportionment percentages of the corporations participating in the study is presented in Table VI. The results for 1957 are in general agreement with the 1957 results for the population. There were some shifts in the direction of the influence of the new formula in 1958 and 1959, but in general the results remained the same.[17] Corporations manufacturing in North Carolina, especially those domiciled there, received reduced apportionment percentages under the new formula more frequently than did corporations selling and not manufacturing in the state.

In Table VII are presented the reasons for the changes, or no change, in the apportionment percentages, or, more accurately inasmuch as some corporations gave more than one reason, the direction of influence of the individual changes in the apportionment formula. Inclusion of the

tions: 73.0 and 72.5, respectively; selling corporations: 60.5 and 57.1, respectively. (*Cf.* Tables V and IX.)

Comparison of the total 1957 tax liabilities of the sample corporations supplying tax data and 1957 data for the population reveals that the sample accurately indicates the direction of change in tax liabilities but not the relative magnitude of the changes. The actual decrease for manufacturing corporations was relatively greater than indicated by the sample, the actual increase for selling corporations relatively less, and the actual decrease for all corporations relatively greater. The percentages indicated by the sample (change related to amount that would have been due had old law remained in effect) and the percentages for the population (change related to the amount that was actually due in the split formula year) were: 6.3 and 14.2 (manufacturing), 8.9 and 4.2 (selling), 2.6 and 9.9 (manufacturing and selling). (Sample: Table VIII; population: Table V and *Statistics of Taxation* [1960], p. 102.) Since the sample consists primarily of corporations affected by the revision, it should, in the absence of the bias, indicate a greater relative change in both directions than actually occurred for all corporations.

17. Six corporations having lower apportionment percentages under the new formula in 1957 had higher percentages under it in 1958; three with higher percentages in 1957 had lower percentages in 1958; one with the same percentage in 1957 had a lower percentage in 1958. There was only one shift between 1958 and 1959: from a higher one in 1958 to a lower one in 1959.

Table VII

INFLUENCE OF REVISIONS IN APPORTIONMENT FORMULA ON
APPORTIONMENT PERCENTAGES OF CORPORATIONS,
BY TYPE OF BUSINESS, 1957

Reason for indicated change in apportionment percentage	NUMBER OF TIMES REASON CITED BY CORPORATIONS		
	Total	Manufacturing	Selling
Increase			
Inclusion of sales factor......................	10	10	—
Change in definition of sales factor..........	13	—	13
Inclusion of payroll factor...................	14	7	7
Inclusion of rental property in property factor.	14	2	12
Application of formula to domestic corporation	1[a]	0	1
Decrease			
Inclusion of sales factor......................	31	31	—
Change in definition of sales factor..........	9	—	9
Inclusion of payroll factor...................	33	5	28
Inclusion of rental property in property factor.	17	3	14
Application of formula to domestic corporation	3[a]	1	2
Vacation of Tax Review Board order........	2	1[b]	1[c]
No change			
Doing business in North Carolina only.......	4	3	1
All sales reported in North Carolina.........	5	5	0
Elected to remain under Tax Review Board order......................	3	1	2

Source: Data obtained from individual corporations by interview and questionnaire.
[a] Most domestic corporations indicated a specific aspect of the new formula rather than this general reason.
[b] Inclusion of sales factor also indicated.
[c] Inclusion of rental property in property factor also indicated.

sales factor for manufacturing firms clearly went in the
direction of reducing their apportionment percentages,
while changing the sales factor from the through offices
to the destination basis for selling firms more often increased their percentages. The strongest single factor
accounting for decreases in the percentages for selling
firms was inclusion of the payroll factor, which in effect
reduced the weight of the sales factor. It was found that
some corporations report all their sales in North Carolina,
though technically they should not. Typically this is a

Table VIII

NORTH CAROLINA INCOME TAX LIABILITIES OF 109
CORPORATIONS UNDER OLD AND NEW LAWS, BY
TYPE OF BUSINESS, 1957, 1958, AND 1959

Amount of tax liability (dollars)	NUMBER OF CORPORATIONS					
	Total		Manufacturing		Selling	
	Old law	New law	Old law	New law	Old law	New law
1957						
0................	4	4	1	1	3	3
1-4,999...........	33	27	8	7	25	20
5,000-9,999.......	13	19	5	7	8	12
10,000-24,999.....	26	30	13	14	13	16
25,000-49,999.....	11	7	6	5	5	2
50,000-99,999.....	6	6	2	2	4	4
100,000-249,999...	13	13	10	9	3	4
250,000-499,999...	1	1	1	1	—	—
500,000-999,999...	—	—	—	—	—	—
1,000,000 & over...	1	1	1	1	—	—
Total number....	108[a]	108	47	47	61	61
Total tax (millions).	$5.27	$5.13	$4.00	$3.75	$1.26	$1.38
1958						
0................	10	10	2	2	8	8
1-4,999...........	31	30	10	10	21	20
5,000-9,999.......	18	19	5	9	13	10
10,000-24,999.....	27	24	16	11	11	13
25,000-49,999.....	6	9	4	5	2	4
50,000-99,999.....	4	6	—	2	4	4
100,000-249,999...	10	9	8	7	2	2
250,000-499,999...	1	—	1	—	—	—
500,000-999,999...	2	1	2	1	—	—
1,000,000 & over...	—	1	—	1	—	—
Total number....	109	109	48	48	61	61
Total tax (millions).	$4.54	$4.28	$3.44	$3.14	$1.10	$1.14
1959						
0................	9	9	3	3	6	6
1-4,999...........	24	19	4	4	20	15
5,000-9,999.......	16	17	5	5	11	12
10,000-24,999.....	24	29	12	14	12	15
25,000-49,999.....	11	9	9	6	2	3
50,000-99,999.....	8	9	3	4	5	5
100,000-249,999...	11	12	7	9	4	3
250,000-499,999...	3	2	3	1	—	1
500,000-999,999...	1	1	1	1	—	—
1,000,000 & over...	1	1	1	1	—	—
Total number....	108[a]	108	48	48	60	60
Total tax (millions).	$6.44	$6.25	$5.01	$4.56	$1.43	$1.68

Source: Data obtained from individual corporations by interview and questionnaire.
[a] One corporation not subject to tax in 1957; tax liability of one not yet settled for 1959.

manufacturing corporation closely held by North Carolinians, whose dividends and securities are exempt from
the state individual income and intangibles taxes to the
extent that the corporate income is taxed by the state.[18]

Table VIII shows comparative tax liabilities under the
old and new formulae for 109 participating corporations
that made the calculations. The 1957 liabilities are those
that would have existed had each formula remained in
effect all year, while the 1958 and 1959 liabilities are those
that would have existed under the old formula and those
that actually arose under the new. Aggregate 1957 tax
liabilities for the sample corporations indicate the known
fact that the new formula reduced the tax liabilities of
manufacturing corporations and increased those of selling
corporations, the net effect being an over-all decrease.[19]
On the basis of 1958 and 1959 sample data, corporate
income tax revenue continues to be less than it would
have been had the law not been revised, with manufacturing corporations paying less and selling corporations
paying more than they would have paid. These effects
are also reflected in the distributions of the individual
corporate tax liabilities, though not very precisely.

More revealing are the distributions of the absolute
and relative changes in tax liabilities (Tables IX, X, and
XI). For a large portion of the corporations affected by
the formula revision, the changes in 1957 tax liabilities
were relatively small: less than 10 per cent for nearly a
third and less than 20 per cent for about half. But some
experienced very substantial changes: for a few tax liabilities were cut in half and for several they were increased
several-fold. Corporations manufacturing in North Caro-

18. The corporate income tax rate is 6 per cent; the individual,
from 3 per cent to 7 per cent, the latter applying to all taxable income
above $10,000. The intangibles rate is 25¢ per $100 market value.
19. See note 16 above.

Table IX

CHANGES IN NORTH CAROLINA INCOME TAX LIABILITIES OF
109 CORPORATIONS, NEW LAW RELATIVE TO OLD LAW,
BY TYPE OF BUSINESS, 1957

Amount and percentage	NUMBER OF CORPORATIONS					
	Total		Manufacturing		Selling	
	Increase	Decrease	Increase	Decrease	Increase	Decrease
Amount (dollars): No change:	12		7		5	
1-499	9	10	2	3	7	7
500-999	3	5	1	—	2	5
1,000-1,999	6	12	2	4	4	8
2,000-2,999	3	3	2	2	1	1
3,000-3,999	1	3	—	—	1	3
4,000-4,999	2	5	1	4	1	1
5,000-7,499	5	4	1	1	4	3
7,500-9,999	1	6	—	3	1	3
10,000-14,999	3	3	1	2	2	1
15,000-24,999	—	1	—	1	—	—
25,000-49,999	—	3	—	3	—	—
50,000-99,999	—	4	—	4	—	—
100,000-149,999	1	2	—	2	1	—
150,000-249,999	—	—	—	—	—	—
250,000-499,999	1	—	1	—	—	—
Totals	35	61	11	29	24	32
Percentage: 0	12		7		5	
1-9	10	19	4	4	6	15
10-19	5	13	1	6	4	7
20-29	3	9	1	5	2	4
30-39	3	12	1	9	2	3
40-49	1	6	—	4	1	2
50-59	1	2	1	1	—	1
60-74	2	—	1	—	1	—
75-99	1	—	1	—	—	—
100-149	2	—	1	—	1	—
150-249	1	—	—	—	1	—
250-499	4	—	—	—	4	—
500 & up	2	—	—	—	2	—
Totals	35	61	11	29	24	32

Source: See Table VIII.

Table X

CHANGES IN NORTH CAROLINA INCOME TAX LIABILITIES OF
109 CORPORATIONS, NEW LAW RELATIVE TO OLD LAW,
BY TYPE OF BUSINESS, 1958

| Amount and percentage | NUMBER OF CORPORATIONS | | | | | |
| | Total | | Manufacturing | | Selling | |
	Increase	Decrease	Increase	Decrease	Increase	Decrease
Amount (dollars):						
No change:	18		8		10	
1-499	7	9	3	1	4	8
500-999	9	8	3	5	6	3
1,000-1,999	4	11	1	3	3	8
2,000-2,999	2	5	1	2	1	3
3,000-3,999	3	3	2	—	1	3
4,000-4,999	3	1	2	1	1	—
5,000-7,499	—	4	—	2	—	2
7,500-9,999	2	3	1	1	1	2
10,000-14,999 ...	4	—	1	—	3	—
15,000-24,999 ...	2	1	—	1	2	—
25,000-49,999 ...	—	3	—	3	—	—
50,000-99,999 ...	—	6	—	6	—	—
100,000-149,999.	—	—	—	—	—	—
150,000-249,999.	1	—	1	—	—	—
Totals	37	54	15	25	22	29
Percentage:						
0	18		8		10	
1-9	10	13	5	3	5	10
10-19	7	16	2	5	5	11
20-29	4	6	3	4	1	2
30-39	3	13	1	9	2	4
40-49	1	6	—	4	1	2
50-59	1	—	1	—	—	—
60-74	1	—	1	—	—	—
75-99	—	—	—	—	—	—
100-149	3	—	2	—	1	—
150-249	1	—	—	—	1	—
250-499	3	—	—	—	3	—
500 & up	3	—	—	—	3	—
Totals	37	54	15	25	22	29

Source: See Table VIII.

Table XI

CHANGES IN NORTH CAROLINA INCOME TAX LIABILITIES OF
109 CORPORATIONS, NEW LAW RELATIVE TO OLD LAW,
BY TYPE OF BUSINESS, 1959

Amount and percentage	NUMBER OF CORPORATIONS					
	Total		Manufacturing		Selling	
	Increase	Decrease	Increase	Decrease	Increase	Decrease
Amount (dollars): No change:	17		9		8	
1-499............	6	10	—	2	6	8
500-999.........	6	8	2	3	4	5
1,000-1,999.....	3	8	—	2	3	6
2,000-2,999.....	2	4	1	2	1	2
3,000-3,999.....	3	3	1	1	2	2
4,000-4,999.....	—	2	—	1	—	1
5,000-7,499......	4	2	3	1	1	1
7,500-9,999.....	2	4	1	2	1	2
10,000-14,999...	3	3	2	3	1	—
15,000-24,999...	3	2	1	—	2	2
25,000-49,999...	1	3	—	3	1	—
50,000-99,999...	—	4	—	4	—	—
100,000-149,999.	—	3	—	3	—	—
150,000-249,999.	1	—	—	—	1	—
250,000-499,999.	1	—	1	—	—	—
Totals........	35	56	12	27	23	29
Percentage: 0	17		9		8	
1-9.............	8	20	2	5	6	15
10-19...........	6	11	1	6	5	5
20-29...........	6	10	5	5	1	5
30-39...........	1	12	—	10	1	2
40-49...........	2	1	1	1	1	—
50-59...........	—	2	—	—	—	2
60-74...........	1	—	—	—	1	—
75-99...........	1	—	1	—	—	—
100-149.........	2	—	1	—	1	—
150-249.........	1	—	1	—	—	—
250-499.........	3	—	—	—	3	—
500 & up........	4	—	—	—	4	—
Totals........	35	56	12	27	23	29

Source: See Table VIII.

lina and selling nationally received a larger share of the substantial decreases than did those only selling in the state, while the latter experienced most of the multiple increases. Based on the experience of the corporations participating in this study, there appears to have been some tendency since 1957 towards a reduction in the larger relative decreases and a slight increase in the larger relative increases. This is true for both manufacturing and selling corporations. It should be noted that the manufacturing corporation that stands out with the greatest tax increase is principally an out-of-state manufacturer selling in the state, but because it has some manufacturing facilities in the state it was classified under the old law as a manufacturing corporation. The fluctuation in the number of sample corporations whose tax liabilities would be unaffected by the revision reflects the fluctuation in the number having no tax liability because of losses.[20]

The aggregate tax liabilities of the participating corporations are juxtaposed in Table XII. The relative difference between the total liabilities of all corporations under the new and old formulae was about the same in 1959 and 1957, but considerably greater in 1958. Based on these three years, it appears that with fluctuations in income, the new formula tends to produce wider fluctuations in tax revenue than would the old. Largely responsible for this is probably the reflection of the destination sales factor in the new formula.

In general, the corporations receiving the greatest benefit in terms of tax relief under the new formula are those firms having a considerable portion of their manufacturing facilties in North Carolina and selling in the

20. Top line, Tables IX, X, and XI. The excess (eight) of the number showing no change in tax liability over the number showing no tax liability represents corporations 100 per cent taxable in North Carolina or filing under Tax Review Board orders.

Table XII

AGGREGATE NORTH CAROLINA INCOME TAX LIABILITIES OF
109 CORPORATIONS UNDER OLD AND NEW LAWS, BY
TYPE OF BUSINESS, 1957, 1958, AND 1959

Year and classification	Aggregate Liabilities		Absolute change (dollars)	Relative change (per cent)
	Old law (dollars)	New law (dollars)		
1957				
Total corporations.....	5,269,098	5,130,171	−138,927	2.64
Mfg. corporations.....	4,004,597	3,751,943	−252,654	6.31
Slg. corporations......	1,264,501	1,378,228	+113,727	8.99
1958				
Total corporations.....	4,536,113	4,281,980	−254,133	5.60
Mfg. corporations.....	3,439,683	3,138,086	−301,597	8.77
Slg. corporations......	1,096,430	1,143,894	+ 47,464	4.33
1959				
Total corporations.....	6,436,064	6,246,727	−189,337	2.94
Mfg. corporations.....	5,006,360	4,562,488	−443,872	8.87
Slg. corporations......	1,429,704	1,684,239	+254,535	17.80

Source: Same as Table VIII.

national market; the ones experiencing the most significant
increases in tax liabilities are those that are wholly or
largely out-of-state manufacturers selling in the state.

EFFECT ON INDIVIDUALS. From the viewpoint of state
revenues in the aggregate, the reduced taxes on corporations were offset to some very small extent by increased
taxes on individuals. While the effect of lower apportionment percentages is to reduce corporate income and
franchise tax liabilities, the effect on individuals is to increase their income and intangibles tax liabilities. This is
due to the fact that dividends and stock values are taxable
under the individual income and intangible property
taxes in the proportion that corporate income is not taxable. The $3.4 million annual reduction in corporate in-

come taxes at the time of the formula revision was offset by perhaps $75,000.[21]

From the viewpoint of particular corporations and the individuals associated therewith, the balance of these two effects would vary, depending upon location of stockholders and dividend policy. There would be no offsetting effect for corporations having no stockholders in North Carolina, while the offsetting effect could, under certain conditions, be more than 100 per cent for a corporation owned exclusively or mostly by North Carolinians (see above, pp. 61-63). For this study, one major manufacturer in the state estimated the over-all effect in its case. Prior to the introduction of the new formula, about 95 per cent of the corporation's income was taxable in North Carolina; afterwards, about 40 per cent. While the corporation is paying over $80,000 less in corporate income taxes, its stockholders are estimated to be paying $21,000 more in individual income taxes and around $12,500 more

21. Let us estimate 7.0 per cent of the income of corporations doing business in North Carolina to be taxable under the old formula and 6.5 per cent taxable under the new (see Table XVIII); thus the percentage taxable for dividends and stock values would be 93.0 and 93.5 per cent under the old and new, respectively. With total net income of corporations doing business in North Carolina around $11 billion ($10.7 billion in 1956, $11.7 billion in 1957, and $9.7 billion in 1958; reported in *Statistics of Taxation* [1958], pp. 137, 177; [1960], pp. 130, 146, 167, 180), the difference in net income apportioned to North Carolina would be $55 million, and the tax on this would be $3.3 million. By taking the property income reported for North Carolina in 1957 (*Survey of Current Business*, XL [August, 1960], p. 21) and assuming that dividends represent the same proportion in North Carolina as in the nation (*ibid.*, XL [July, 1960], p. 15), it is estimated that North Carolinians received $180 million in dividends. The above increase in the percentage taxable would add $.9 million to taxable income, taxed at 3 to 7 per cent, the latter applying to individual taxable income above $10,000. Applying 6 per cent to the $.9 million addition gives $54,000. The intangible property tax on shares of stock yielded $3.5 million in the fiscal year 1957-58 (*Statistics of Taxation* [1958], p. 262); the above increase in the percentage taxable would add $17,500. (Collections from the intangibles tax are distributed to the local governments.)

INTERSTATE APPORTIONMENT

Table XIII

REACTIONS OF CORPORATIONS TO NORTH CAROLINA
PROPERTY-PAYROLL-SALES FORMULA, BY TYPE
OF CORPORATION AND TYPE OF BUSINESS

Reaction	NUMBER OF CORPORATIONS EXPRESSING ENUMERATED REACTIONS								
	All			Domestic			Foreign		
	Total	Mfg.	Slg.	Total	Mfg.	Slg.	Total	Mfg.	Slg.
Satisfied									
No further comment..........	14	6	8	6	4	2	8	2	6
Fairly represents business done within state...............	11	5	6	1	1	0	10	4	6
More equitable than old.......	9	5	4	2	1	1	7	4	3
Furthers uniformity among states......................	8	6	2	0	0	0	8	6	2
Reasonable or basically fair....	6	1	5	0	0	0	6	1	5
Changed definition of sales an improvement...............	4	1	3	1	1	0	3	0	3
Formula includes major income producing elements..........	4	1	3	1	0	1	3	1	2
Reduces tax liability..........	4	2	2	1	1	0	3	1	2
Income may be apportioned to non-income tax states.......	1	1	0	1	1	0	0	0	0
Reasonably satisfied...........	2	1	1	1	1	0	1	0	1
Equally satisfied with old or new	2	2	0	1	1	0	1	1	0
	65	31	34	15	11	4	50	20	30
Satisfied except for:									
Changed definition of sales.....	6	3	3	0	0	0	6	3	3
Exclusion of executive salaries in payroll factor............	2	1	1	0	0	0	2	1	1
Definition of sales (in interest of uniformity)..............	1	1	0	0	0	0	1	1	0
Treatment of earnings of subsidiaries.................	2	2	0	0	0	0	2	2	0
Apportionment of some income from intangibles............	1	1	0	0	0	0	1	1	0
	12	8	4	0	0	0	12	8	4
Dissatisfied									
Destination basis for sales factor objectionable.........	4	0	4	0	0	0	4	0	4
Definition of sales not in interest of uniformity........	1	0	1	0	0	0	1	0	1
Unreasonably large attribution of income to N.C............	4	1	3	0	0	0	4	1	3

Table XIII continued

Reaction	NUMBER OF CORPORATIONS EXPRESSING ENUMERATED REACTIONS								
	All			Domestic			Foreign		
	Total	Mfg.	Slg.	Total	Mfg.	Slg.	Total	Mfg.	Slg.
Causes 100+% of income to be taxed.....................	1	0	1	1	0	1	0	0	0
Old formula more equitable....	1	1	0	0	0	0	1	1	0
Increases tax liability..........	2	1	1	0	0	0	2	1	1
Separate accounting preferable..	3	1	2	0	0	0	3	1	2
Property-sales formula preferable	2	0	2	0	0	0	2	0	2
Property (excluding rentals)-sales formula preferable......	2	0	2	0	0	0	2	0	2
Property-payroll formula preferable..................	1	0	1	0	0	0	1	0	1
Treatment of federal income taxes and earnings of subsidiaries objectionable........	1	0	1	0	0	0	1	0	1
	22	4	18	1	0	1	21	4	17
No answer..................	27	17	10	11	8	3	16	9	7
Total corporations........	126	60	66	27	19	8	99	41	58

Source: Data obtained from individual corporations by interview and questionnaire.

in intangible personal property taxes. Of course, North Carolina stockholders of corporations paying more taxes under the new formula are paying less.

Reactions of Corporations to New Formula

About one-half of the participating corporations, or two-thirds of those expressing an opinion, are satisfied with the property-payroll-sales formula used by North Carolina (Table XIII). The majority of the comments of the satisfied involved the general fairness or accuracy of apportionment. The dissatisfied also referred to fairness and accuracy, but they tended to single out the particular cause of their dissatisfaction, which was most often the destination sales factor. Certainly the strongest and most vehement comments were aimed at this object.

There were a few exceptions, but in general those satisfied with the new formula were enjoying lower taxes and the dissatisfied were incurring higher taxes under it.

With only one exception, the domestic firms were satisfied with the new arrangement.

The Actual Effects: Industrialization

Over the past third of a century numerous studies have been made in an attempt to determine the relationship between taxation and industrial development. The methods employed include questionnaires, interviews, correlation analysis, the hypothetical tax bill approach, and even "motivational" research.[22] On the whole, the studies support the general position that the tax factor is one of a host of minor factors, ranking behind the major fac-

22. Examples: (1) questionnaire and interview: Policyholders Service Bureau of the Metropolitan Life Insurance Company and the Civic Development Committee of the National Electric Light Association, *Industrial Development in the United States and Canada* (New York, 1928); Glenn E. McLaughlin and Stefan Robock, *Why Industry Moves South* (Washington: NPA, 1949); (2) correlation analysis: G. L. Leffler and H. M. Groves, *Wisconsin Industry and the Wisconsin Tax System* (Madison: University of Wisconsin Bureau of Business and Economic Research, 1931); C. C. Bloom, *State and Local Tax Differentials* (Iowa City: Bureau of Business Research, State University of Iowa, 1955); (3) hypothetical tax bill approach: Joe S. Floyd, Jr., *Effects of Taxation on Industrial Location* (Chapel Hill: University of North Carolina Press, 1952). For a review of these and other studies, see James W. Martin and William G. Herzel, "The Influence of Taxation Upon Industrial Development," *State Government*, XXX (July, 1957), pp. 145-49, 164-65, and John F. Due, "Studies of State-Local Tax Influences on Location of Industry," *National Tax Journal*, XIV (June, 1961), pp. 163-73. See also *A Survey of State Planning and Development Programs* (Chapel Hill: University of North Carolina School of Business Administration, 1960; mimeographed). Interviews in depth have been conducted by the Survey Research Center of the Institute for Social Research at the University of Michigan; see Harvey E. Brazer, "Taxation and Industrial Location in Michigan," in W. Haber, *et al.*, *The Michigan Economy* (Kalamazoo: The W. E. Upjohn Institute for Employment Research, 1959), p. 323.

tors of manpower, markets, and materials, in determining industrial development. The studies have shown that, for most firms, state and local taxes are not a major cost element and that significant tax differentials may be largely offset by significant differentials in public services. Generally, the tax factor can be decisive only when all other factors are equal.

There is no intention to include here any scientific and exhaustive study of the relationship between taxation and industrial development. However, in light of the Tax Commission's hopes regarding the effect of the change in North Carolina's income tax law on industrial development, it is appropriate to present any available evidence pertaining to the influence of this change on location decisions.

In an attempt to get some idea of the extent to which the change in the apportionment formula has influenced industrial location, inquiries were addressed to senior officials of 40 major corporations that had, from 1958 to 1960, located or proposed the location of new or expanded facilities in North Carolina.[23] Replies were received from 35, with 33, or 82.5 per cent, furnishing data. Of these, only one indicated that the 1957 revision influenced the location decision, one was uncertain, and 31 indicated that it did not influence their decisions. Twenty-six of these 31 indicated that this could be taken to mean that they would have made the same decision, other things being the same, had the law remained as it was before 1957; one, that it could not be so taken; and four did not answer.

23. Names of the corporations were obtained from the Division of Commerce and Industry, North Carolina Department of Conservation and Development, which each year releases a list entitled "New and Proposed Industries—Reported for North Carolina." Names of senior officials were obtained from Moody's *Industrial Manual* (1960). Along with a personal letter addressed to the official was sent a questionnaire.

Table XIV

RANKING OF THE IMPORTANCE OF FACTORS BY 31 FIRMS MAKING LOCATION DECISIONS

Factor	NUMBER OF CORPORATIONS ASSIGNING SPECIFIED RANKS													
	1	2	3	4	5	6	7	8	9	10	11	12	13	14
Markets	12	2	1		1									
Manpower	4	3	3	1	1	3								
Momentum of early start	3	4	1											
Materials	2	1	1				1						1	
Building construction costs	2		3	2					1					
Manufacturing space immediately available	2													
Transportation facilities	1	4	3	2	1		2			1				
Land cost and availability	1	4	1	3	1		1				1			
Power and fuel	1	1	1				1							
Living conditions	1		1		2	2			1					
Capital availability	1		1							2				
Climate	1					1	1	1	1					
Unionization of labor		3				1		1						
Water supply		2	1											1
Diversification for national defense		2						1						
Complementary industries		1		1										
Service industries		1					1	1						
Waste disposal				1	2				1					
Educational systems			1	1	1			1				1		
Taxes, local				1	2				1		1			
Financial aids				1	1									
Taxes, state			1	1		1		1						
Personal reasons						1								
Religious and cultural advantages						1								
Certainty of government policy							1							
Recreational facilities						1								
Totals	31	28	19	14	12	11	8	6	5	3	2	1	1	1

Source: Data obtained from individual corporations by questionnaire.

Of the 33 corporations responding, 31 made some attempt at listing, in order of importance, the factors upon which the decision to locate or expand in North Carolina was based.[24] Table XIV shows the ranks given the vari-

24. These 31 firms are classified as follows: electrical machinery, equipment, and supplies, 6; chemicals and allied products, 5; food and kindred products, 5; fabricated metals, 4; machinery (except electrical), 4; textile mill products, 3; primary metals, 2; apparel, 1; rubber products, 1.

ous factors by the firms. Most listed only a few factors: for example, less than half (14 of 31) listed four or more factors. Three indicated only one factor: one stated that the immediate availability of manufacturing space was the main reason for locating an operation in North Carolina; the other two stated that the factors they indicated, market in one case and momentum of early start in the other, were the reasons for locating and expanding in these particular locations. The results shown in the table appear to conform with the results that would be expected

Table XV

RANKS OF FACTORS IN LOCATION DECISIONS
OF FIVE FIRMS

Factor	Firm[a]				
	A	B	C	D	E
Building construction costs...	1	—	—	4	3
Capital availability..........	—	—	—	—	10
Climate...................	—	—	—	9	—
Diversification for national defense...............	2	—	—	8	—
Educational systems........	3	—	—	6	—
Financial aids.............	—	—	—	—	4
Land cost and availability....	—	2	—	—	5
Living conditions..........	—	—	—	5	6
Manpower................	4	6	3	1	1
Markets..................	—	1	—	3	—
Materials.................	—	—	—	13	—
Momentum of early start....	—	—	1	—	—
Power and fuel............	—	—	—	2	—
Service industries..........	—	—	—	7	—
Taxes, local...............	5	4	5	12	9
Taxes, state...............	6	5	—	11	8
Transportation............	—	3	—	10	7
Certainty of government policy.................	7	—	—	—	—
Unionization of labor........	8	—	—	—	2
Waste disposal.............	9	—	4	—	—
Water supply..............	—	—	2	14	—

Source: Data obtained from individual corporations by questionnaire.
[a] All firms are manufacturers: A, D, and E, electrical machinery and equipment; B, machinery other than electrical; C, textile mill products.

on the basis of the numerous theoretical and empirical analyses made in this area.

The tax factor itself appears to have played a very minor role in these location decisions. Only five firms mentioned local taxes and only four, state taxes; no firm ranked either higher than fourth. Table XV shows the individual rankings made by the five firms that indicated taxes to be a factor. Taxes ranked near the bottom of the list for all firms except one (A),[25] and it appears that its official was possibly influenced by the alphabetical listing of the factors on the questionnaire.[26]

Among the 126 firms referred to above in connection with the revenue effects, two indicated that the formula change had influenced their location decisions.[27] One stated that the formula revision was a factor considered in the decision to expand the plant. The other, which refused to release tax data, claimed that a multi-million dollar expansion planned for another state was shifted to North Carolina as a result of the formula revision. Officials of this large manufacturing firm assert that the firm, because of this shift, is now paying more North Carolina income taxes under the new formula than it would be paying if the formula had not been changed.

The views of the 126 firms regarding the importance of the tax factor in the location of economic activity are presented in Table XVI. Of the ones answering the question, about a ninth views the tax factor as primary, while about a sixth attaches no significance to it. There exists

25. Because of the number of factors listed, the same rank has different meanings for each firm.

26. Or perhaps he made no attempt to list them in the order of importance. In only one other case where three or more factors were listed were they in alphabetical order, and these were markets, materials, and transportation for a firm in the milling industry.

27. There is an overlap of nine firms between the two groups, but the two referred to here are not in the group of 33.

Table XVI

COMMENTS OF CORPORATIONS ON IMPORTANCE OF TAX
FACTOR IN LOCATION OF ECONOMIC ACTIVITY,
BY TYPE OF BUSINESS

Comment	NUMBER OF CORPORATIONS MAKING COMMENT		
	Total	Manufacturing	Selling
I			
No significance........................	10	5	5
Unimportant; not even tertiary............	2	1	1
Moves not influenced by tax factor.........	1	1	0
	13	7	6
II			
Relatively minor........................	11	8	3
Only one of many factors.................	10	4	6
One of many, but may be determining.......	6	3	3
Purely secondary factor..................	5	2	3
Secondary, but could be determining........	2	0	2
Final determining factor after all others......	1	0	1
Only a grossly disproportionate tax burden significant..................	1	0	1
	36	17	19
III			
Influences decisions; taken into consideration.	6	4	2
Important, but not primary...............	4	4	0
One of many important factors............	3	1	2
Total tax package significant..............	3	1	2
	16	10	6
IV			
A major factor; primary importance........	5	1	4
Matter of substantial consideration.........	2	1	1
Tax climate a most important consideration..	2	1	1
	9	3	6
V			
Tax factor becoming more important........	3	1	2
Assurance of equitable treatment more important than amount.............	1	1	0
Income tax not significant because of continual changes in laws............	1	0	1
Local taxes more important than state income taxes.....................	1	1	0
	6	3	3
VI			
No answer............................	46	20	26
Total corporations............	126	60	66

Source: Data obtained from individual corporations by interview and questionnaire.

Table XVII

RATIO OF CORPORATE INCOME TAXES DUE NORTH CAROLINA
TO CORPORATE PROFITS IN THE UNITED STATES, 1950-1959

Year	Corporate profits before tax (millions of dollars) (1)	Corporate income taxes due North Carolina (thousands of dollars) (2)	Per cent (2) is of (1) (3)
1950............	40,628	39,415	.0970
1951............	42,153	42,050	.0998
1952............	36,691	35,385	.0964
1953............	38,311	36,073	.0942
1954............	34,061	33,946	.0997
1955............	44,862	43,037	.0959
1956............	44,683	44,972	.1006
1957............	43,208	41,822	.0968
1958............	37,698	37,592	.0997
1959............	47,021	48,846ᵃ	.1039

Source: Corporate profits: "National Income and Product in 1959," *Survey of Current Business*, XL (July, 1960), p. 8; North Carolina corporate income tax liabilities: *Statistics of Taxation* (1956), p. 100; (1960), p. 102; North Carolina corporate income tax collections, *ibid.* p. 97.
ᵃ Tax liability data for 1959 not yet available; tax collections for the fiscal year 1959-60 used instead.

a wide range of viewpoints in between, but the most prevalent viewpoint is that the factor is secondary or minor.

The period since the change is probably too short to ascertain any changes in the rate of industrialization in the state relative to the rate for the region or the nation, even if causes of any changes could be identified. However, it is interesting to note that the percentage of corporate profits in the nation owed to North Carolina in the form of corporate income taxes has remained very stable over the past decade (Table XVII). In fact, if the percentages are rounded to a hundredth of a per cent, they are .10 for every year except 1953 (.09). The fact that the percentages are as high for the period after the formula revision as for the preceding period may indicate that industrial development in the state has offset the effect of lower apportionment percentages. Table XVIII shows,

Table XVIII

RATIO OF NET INCOME TAXABLE IN NORTH CAROLINA TO
TOTAL NET INCOME OF CORPORATIONS FILING NORTH
CAROLINA RETURNS, BY TYPE OF CORPORATION,
1950-1958

Year	PERCENT OF NET INCOME TAXABLE IN NORTH CAROLINA		
	All corporations	Domestic corporations	Foreign corporations
1950.................	7.98	96.08	4.19
1951.................	8.12	95.35	4.00
1952.................	8.48	95.53	4.64
1953.................	6.77	95.52	3.86
1954.................	6.90	96.25	4.14
1955.................	6.10	95.63	3.60
1956.................	7.00	97.20	4.08
1957.................	5.95	92.01	3.52
1958.................	6.43	88.42	3.77

Source: Calculated from data appearing in Tables 48, 51, 56, and 60 of *Statistics of Taxation* (1960), and corresponding tables of *Statistics of Taxation* (1952, 1954, 1956, and 1958). The magnitude of the figures from which the percentages were calculated is indicated by data for 1958: domestic corporations reported total net income of $305.9 million, of which $270.5 million was apportioned to North Carolina; foreign corporations filing in North Carolina reported $9.4 billion and $356.1 million; all corporations, $9.7 billion and $626.5 million.

for corporations filing North Carolina returns, that the per cent of their total net income taxable in North Carolina was lower in 1957 and 1958 than in the earlier years of the 1950's. The number of returns filed increased every year during the period.[28]

Conclusion

The apparent harshness of the North Carolina tax structure as it applied to industry was largely removed by the 1957 legislation. This was accomplished, not by the particular apportionment formula adopted, but by giving equal treatment to domestic and foreign corporations, by

28. From 11,378 in 1950 to 17,629, in 1958. For 1956, 1957, and 1958, the numbers were 16,032, 16,887, and 17,629, respectively. In 1958 returns were filed by over 15,000 domestic and over 2,000 foreign corporations. (*Statistics of Taxation* [1960], p. 99; [1958], p. 99; [1956], p. 97; [1954], p. 95.)

applying the same formula to multi-state businesses irrespective of their principal business within the state, and by separately allocating non-unitary income. North Carolina may still be regarded by some as a "high tax" state because of the relatively high tax rate and the disallowance of federal income tax deduction, but these features would hardly be classified as inequities. Some corporations are still filing under special formulae granted by the Tax Review Board before 1957 and paying lower taxes than they would pay under the new statutory formula. In the interest of assuring equitable treatment, these orders, in the opinion of the author, should have been rescinded in 1957 and any of these corporations regarding the new formula as inequitable in their situations should have been required to file new petitions for special treatment. Furthermore, the actions of the Board should be made a matter of public record.

As for the cost of this revision in terms of revenue loss, the reduction in revenue was about half that anticipated by the Tax Study Commission, and the number of corporations experiencing tax increases relative to those experiencing decreases was considerably greater than anticipated. The principal reason for this is the fact that the destination sales factor was seriously underestimated in the calculations.

The revision affected the tax liabilities of only 6 per cent of the corporations filing returns, and for most of these the change in liabilities was relatively small. However, for some the changes were very substantial, a larger share of the substantial decreases going to North Carolina manufacturers selling nationally and most of the several-fold increases going to out-of-state manufacturers selling in North Carolina.

In the aggregate, corporate income tax revenue continues to be less than it would have been had the law not been revised. However, the percentage of corporate profits before taxes in the nation being paid to North Carolina in the form of income taxes has remained amazingly stable. This may indicate that industrial growth has offset the effects of the formula revision, but the change in the formula appears to have had little effect on location decisions. Among 33 major firms deciding to locate or expand facilities in North Carolina from 1958 to 1960, only one indicated that the 1957 formula revision influenced its decision, and none ranked state and local taxes relatively high in the list of factors entering its decision. Among the total of 150 firms participating in the study (the 33 in the location sample, plus 117 in the revenue sample that were not also in the location sample), three indicated that the revision had influenced a location decision, one claiming it was the decisive factor. Generally, the tax factor is of minor or secondary importance in the location decisions of these corporate officials.

For the limited period for which data are available, it appears that the new formula produces, with fluctuations in economic activity, wider fluctuations in tax revenue than did the old formula.

Chapter V

Economic Analysis: Apportionment

Introduction

It was pointed out in the above case study that certain inequities in the North Carolina apportionment method were corrected by eliminating discriminatory treatment based on corporate domicile and nature of business activity. The particular formula adopted affected tax liabilities individually and in the aggregate, but the correction of the inequities did not depend upon the formula. The purpose of this chapter is to analyze the apportionment of business income with the aim of suggesting a formula that is theoretically sound and practical. The analysis is in terms of economics, rather than law or accounting as is traditionally the case in this area.

Theory of Business Taxation

The principal reason for the taxation of business is that business units are a convenient source of substantial revenue. However, many justifications are advanced: the provision by government of general and special benefits to business, the existence of social costs attributable to business operations, the desirability of regulating or controlling certain types of business activity, and the alleged ability-to-pay on the part of business units. To justify the taxation of corporation income, the same reasons are advanced, plus another: the necessity for a corporate income tax to prevent the use of the corporation as an instrument for avoiding the personal income tax.

Varying degrees of validity may be attached to the preceding reasons or justifications, but a crucial question is: Who bears the burden of the corporate income tax? Traditionally, economic theory has shown how an income tax on pure profit cannot be shifted. But when account is taken of the fact that the corporate net income tax is on business profit, not economic or pure profit, theory shows that some shifting can occur. When further account is taken of such "facts of life" as imperfect competition, "full-cost" pricing, inflationary trends, and anti-competitive agreements, even part of the tax on economic profit might be shifted. Conclusions of the various analytical and empirical studies recently made vary from one extreme to the other, but the majority find that some of the corporate income tax is shifted.[1] The fact that the rate of return on investment after taxes in manufacturing follows an almost level trend line over the past several decades seems to be evidence that, in the long run, corporate income taxes are not borne by the owners.[2]

As for the incidence of state corporate income taxes, isolated from the total, two factors may operate, one increasing and the other reducing the degree of shifting as compared with the federal. The former is the existence in several states of a supplementary capital stock tax that establishes a minimum tax liability for corporations earn-

1. For a survey of a representative group of the studies, see B. U. Ratchford and P. B. Han, "The Burden of the Corporate Income Tax," *National Tax Journal*, X (December, 1957), pp. 310-24.

2. See Eugene M. Lerner and Eldon S. Hendricksen, "Federal Taxes on Corporate Income and the Rate of Return on Investment in Manufacturing, 1927 to 1952," *National Tax Journal*, IX (September, 1956), pp. 193-202.

ing no net income.[3]   The latter comes into play in the case of directly competing firms located in different states that impose different tax burdens.

If corporate income taxes were borne exclusively by the owners, the tax would probably be roughly progressive.   In actual practice, however, the burden seems to be borne variously: by consumers, by employees and suppliers, and by the owners.   The equity of such a haphazard distribution of the tax burden as this can be seriously questioned.   However, it is a part of the over-all tax structure, capitalized into many decisions already made, and to make radical changes would be an "egg-unscrambling" task.[4]

Theory of Apportionment

In taxing the net income of corporations, a state faces, with respect to those businesses also operating in other states, the problem of determining the portion of net income that is attributable to that state.   If a multi-state corporation's business within a state is truly separate and distinct from its business without the state, then separate accounting provides a theoretically and practically sound method for determining the net income earned within the state.   However, if the business of the multi-state corporation is unitary, as is most often the case, separate accounting is unsound, the concepts of separate accounting and unitary business being incompatible.   Inconsistent with economic unity, separate accounting for unitary businesses would be fraught with arbitrariness and difficulty in the geographical allocation of gross income and

3. See William J. Shultz and C. Lowell Harriss, *American Public Finance* (6th ed.; New York: Prentice-Hall, 1954), p. 347.

4. For an evaluation of corporate taxation, particularly the taxation of undistributed profits, and an argument for an expenditure tax, see Nicholas Kaldor, *An Expenditure Tax* (London: George Allen & Unwin Ltd., 1955), especially Chapter V, entitled "Company Taxation."

certain expenses and in the setting of intrafirm transfer prices. Furthermore, it would involve higher administrative and compliance costs than do some other methods of income apportionment.[5]

At the opposite pole from separate accounting is the apportionment of the total income by some statutory formula. This treatment presents legal and theoretical difficulties with respect to non-unitary income that may be earned by the business. There is a good case for separately allocating the items of income not directly connected with the main business of the firm and the expenses related to these items. This is generally provided for in state income tax laws, but among the states there is some diversity as to the specific items to be directly allocated and considerable diversity as to the bases on which the items are assigned.[6]

In between separate accounting and complete apportionment by formula is the procedure generally followed: direct allocation of non-unitary net income and apportionment by formula of unitary net income. Of course, the major part of corporate income is unitary[7] and thus subject to apportionment by formula.

The rationale for using a formula consisting of a few factors to apportion unitary income is that the income is created by numerous means of production spread through-

5. See above, p. 24, and n. 47.
6. See Albert H. Cohen, *Apportionment and Allocation Formulae and Factors Used by States in Levying Taxes Based on or Measured by Net Income of Manufacturing, Distributive and Extractive Corporations* (New York: Controllership Foundation, Inc., 1954), pp. 9-13, 53-58; Prentice-Hall, Inc., *State and Local Tax Service,* pp. 1039-40, dated June 7, 1960; above, p. 31.
7. For example, for foreign corporations taxable in North Carolina in 1958, income subject to direct allocation amounted to $1.3 billion, $.9 million to North Carolina, and income subject to apportionment by formula amounted to $7.9 billion, $.3 billion to North Carolina. (*Statistics of Taxation* [1960], p. 181.)

out the area in which the firm operates, but it is not feasible to attempt to apportion the income on the basis of the location of all these means. The task would be Herculean, and, incidentally, some of the means of production would have to be apportioned by formula. To make the task manageable, the income is apportioned on the basis of the location of a few major factors. Analysis of the factors to be included is in the next section below.

The foregoing approach to the apportionment of unitary income might be referred to as the contribution-to-income approach. Another conceivable approach is from the viewpoint of the burden of the corporate income tax: burden-of-tax approach. If it were proved that the burden of the corporate income tax rests exclusively on the owners, then the states might carve up a corporation's net income on the basis of the residence of its stockholders, each state applying its rate to its portion. (This theory of the distribution of the burden seems to underlie the provision of the North Carolina law exempting dividends under the individual income tax in the proportion that the corporation's income is taxed under the corporate income tax.) Similarly, if the tax burden rests exclusively on employees or on purchasers, the apportionment of income might be based on the location of payrolls or customers. However, if the tax were shifted in accordance with one of these simple models, the states could, under more simplified tax structures, capture the revenue with their individual income taxes or sales taxes, assuming they were employing these taxes. In the real world, of course, the tax is shifted in various directions; all states do not tax corporate income; states taxing corporate income have different definitions of taxable income and different rates; some states have supplementary capital stock taxes; the significance of the limited jurisdiction of states varies among corporations; and so forth. Again emerges the picture of a haphazard distribution of the tax burden among individuals.

A Theoretically Sound and Practical Formula

BURDEN-OF-TAX APPROACH. If objective data on the distribution of the burden of the corporate income tax could be obtained, it would be relatively simple to work out an apportionment formula from the burden-of-tax approach. Assuming that the burden is borne by consumers, employees, and stockholders, the formula could consist of three factors: sales, payroll, and equity capital, weighted in accordance with the portion of the tax borne by each group of individuals. It must be noted, though, that this would not be so accurate or precise as taxing the individuals directly under state individual income and sales taxes, because with differences among the states in such things as tax rates the amount of tax revenue exacted by a state from a corporation would not necessarily equal the amount of tax shifted to or borne by individuals within that state.[8] Furthermore, control over distributive justice is lacking in the case of the corporate income tax, the tax being distributed among individuals with little, if any, reference to their ability to pay.

Compared with the widely used property-payroll-sales formula, a formula arrived at from the burden-of-tax

8. For example, assume a corporation operating and selling in two states and owned by the citizens of those two states. Its sales are evenly divided between the two areas, but 90 per cent of the employees live in State A and 70 per cent of the stock is owned by A residents. Assume that the tax is borne completely and equally by consumers, employees, and owners. The tax laws of States A and B are identical, except A's rate is 3 per cent and B's is 6 per cent. Using a uniform three-factor formula, A apportions 70 per cent of the corporation's $100 net income to A, and B apportions 30 per cent to B. A's tax revenue is $2.10 (.03 × $70); B's $1.80 (.06 × $30). However, the total tax of $3.90 is distributed $2.73 to A residents and $1.17 to B residents.

approach would possess no practical advantages. The sales factor must be contended with in either, and the equity capital factor would involve more problems than the tangible property factor. Moreover, an additional factor, purchases, might have to be included in the burden-of-tax formula if it were found that suppliers bear a significant portion of the corporate income tax. Of course, if it were found that the tax is borne completely by consumers, then the one-factor burden-of-tax formula would be simpler, but it would consist of the most trouble-some factor in the three-factor formula. Theoretically, the burden-of-tax formula would possess one major advantage: the use of the destination sales factor can be justified under this approach. But the approach can hardly be justified, inasmuch as it amounts to an indirect, haphazard method of taxing individual incomes and sales.

CONTRIBUTION-TO-INCOME APPROACH. To determine how corporate profits might be apportioned from the viewpoint of the location of the factors contributing to net income, an understanding of the nature and sources of profit would seem essential. Traditionally in economic theory pure profit is viewed as a residual return: the excess of income over all economic costs, including explicit costs, implicit costs, and rents of monopoly positions. With this definition, the source of pure profit is uncertainty, profit arising because of innovations and because of changes in markets and the general environment. Profit can then be defined as the difference between expected receipts and actual receipts or between *ex ante* income and *ex post* income.[9]

9. See J. Fred Weston, "A Generalized Uncertainty Theory of Profit," *American Economic Review*, XL (March, 1950), pp. 40-60, and John F. Due, *Intermediate Economic Analysis* (Homewood, Ill.: Irwin, 1956), p. 444. This profit theory is concerned with profit as an element in individual incomes. For a discussion of profit as a distributive share

The classical concept of profit as a combination of the entrepreneur's wages, interest, and risk indemnity fits fairly well for the small proprietorship or partnership, but for the large corporation the concept of pure profit presented in the preceding paragraph is relevant. To a large degree the costs that are implicit in a proprietorship or partnership are explicit in a corporation. Also, the concept of profit as a functional return fits fairly well for the small proprietorship or partnership, but for the large corporation profit is better described as a residual return. With the separation of ownership and management in the large corporation, pure profits accrue largely to individuals not performing the entrepreneurial functions.

If the corporate income tax were applied to pure profit, it would be practically impossible to construct an apportionment formula from the contribution-to-income approach. The task would be to locate geographically the sources of pure profit: such factors as a new method of production, a new advertising technique, a fluctuation in general economic activity, or a change in government policy. If the tax were applied to both pure profit and monopoly profit (the excess of income over explicit costs and implicit costs), the task would be to locate geographically such additional sources as exploitation in imperfect markets, patents, and goodwill.

Actually the tax is levied against neither of these concepts of profit, but against business profit (the excess of income over explicit costs, including depreciation). Since business or accounting profit is higher than pure or economic profit to the extent that implicit costs and rents of monopoly positions[10] are included in the former,

(aggregate profit) and the relation of profit as a distributive share to macroeconomics, see Richard M. Davis, "The Current State of Profit Theory," *American Economic Review*, XLII (June, 1952), pp. 245-64.

10. Rents of monopoly positions are similar to implicit costs from

the aggregate tax revenue is higher and more firms have tax liabilities than they would if the tax were levied against economic profit. If the economy were purely competitive and static, no revenue would be raised by a tax levied against either economic profit or against both economic and monopoly profits, for these two types of profit arise as the result of dynamic forces operating in the economy and the existence of non-purely competitive market conditions. To ferret out and locate geographically the sources of business profit, which would include pure profit, monopoly profit, and implicit costs, would be practically impossible. Even if it could be done, the results would vary immensely among industries and among firms within the same industry. Consider, for example, the difference in the explanations for profits in the pharmaceutical industry and the steel industry.[11]

The above conclusions can be included with other points such as distributive injustice and the effects on consumption, investment, and capital structures in the case against business taxation. But, with corporate income being taxed, there is—under the contribution-to-income approach—an alternative attack that yields a theoretically sound and practical formula. Its relevance is especially apparent when account is taken of the fact that corporate income taxes are very generally regarded by corporate officials as costs. The federal government allows corporations to deduct state income taxes in arriving at taxable income, and about half the states levying corporate income taxes allow the deductibility of the federal income tax. For a firm to continue in busi-

the viewpoint of the firm, but the two are different in that the former do not ration resources among competing uses.

11. See Peter L. Bernstein, "Profit Theory—Where Do We Go from Here?" *Quarterly Journal of Economics*, LXVII (August, 1953), pp. 412-13.

ness, all costs must be covered by income (output). The question is: What produces this income (output)? The answer is, of course, the factors or means of production. The problem, then, is to locate these means spatially in order that the income might be apportioned among the states as the means are distributed.

In our fairly competitive economy, the best indication of the contributions of the various means is the amount of money spent for them. The distribution of a firm's expenditures among the states would be the basis for apportioning its net income. The formula used by a corporation would be a simple expense formula: expenses incurred in state A to total expenses; there would be no problem of weighting several factors. Labor costs would be allocated on the basis of the place where service is performed; material purchases, on the basis of origin; property costs such as depreciation, interest, and property taxes, on the basis of location of the property. Of course, some costs would be troublesome: for example, national advertising. Theoretically, the expense formula is sound. But practically there are difficulties. On the one hand, there would be compliance and administrative problems such as increased record-keeping, particularly with respect to purchases, the possibility of manipulation of expense location, and the legal problem of allocating income to states lacking jurisdiction to tax. On the other, it would be a sharp departure from the formulae now used.

By a little streamlining, however, the expense formula can be converted into a formula that is still theoretically sound and more practical than the ones now used. In broad terms, income is produced by the factors land, labor, and capital. Payroll data, which are readily available, furnish the amount spent on labor and can be fairly easily allocated among the states. Property values, which are readily available, indicate the value of services performed by land and capital, practically all of which are easily located. Of the 37 states taxing corporate income, 33 employ a property factor in their formulae and 31 a payroll or manufacturing cost factor (see Table II above). With payrolls measured in terms of payments and property in terms of values, the weight given each when combined must be selected. Since compensation of employees accounts for over two-thirds of the national income, the weights could logically be two or three (payrolls) and one (property). It is realized that the payroll factor generally "follows" the property factor, as in manufacturing operations, but there are instances where it diverges, as in the case of traveling salesmen. Though it may be argued that the property-payroll weighting should be more nearly equal, inasmuch as there are wide variations among industries in the importance of property relative to labor, it is essential to assure that labor devoted to selling activities receives "full weight." Of course, each corporation could be required to use unique weights based on some relationship between its aggregate payroll and property figures.

The property-payroll formula is not only theoretically sound, but it is relatively simple and certain, is fairly easily complied with and administered, and, relative to formulae now in use, would adversely affect resource allocation and economic development to a smaller degree. If simplicity possesses high priority, the labor factor could be measured by the number of employees located in each state, with no account being taken of differences in compensation.

The formula proposed here is different from the one most widely used in that it does not contain a sales factor. If income is to be apportioned on the basis of the location of the factors creating the income, inclusion of a sales factor cannot be economically justified. Granted, selling is a function in the income-creating process, but its relative position among other functions should be indicated by the labor and property devoted to selling, not by sales. In fact, with a sales factor included in the formula, the labor and property devoted to selling are allocated once in the payroll and property factors, and then the sales factor in effect allows them to be counted again, at a much heavier weight. The sales factor may also be condemned on the economic grounds that it interferes with the allocation of resources, increasing the real cost of goods, by inducing firms to manipulate their selling operations for tax advantages and by imposing upon them more work in compliance.

The strongest objections to the property-payroll formula are raised by those favoring a destination basis sales factor.[12] Their general argument is that without the market there would be no income to be taxed. This is true, just as a three-legged stool falls upon the removal of any one leg. But the property-payroll formula does not exclude consideration of the market: the market is considered to the extent that income-producing activities are carried on in the market area. Of course, they are arguing that the market should be given more consideration than this, but more consideration cannot be economically justified under the contribution-to-income approach. As shown above, it might be justified under the burden-of-tax approach, but this leads to the conclusion that the appropriate tax is probably a sales tax rather than a corporate income tax. Some of the destination sales factor advocates argue that the seller is "exploiting" the market. They may be overlooking the fact, however, that con-

12. See above, pp. 27-28.

Table XIX

NORTH CAROLINA INCOME TAX LIABILITIES OF 104 CORPORATIONS UNDER PROPERTY-PAYROLL-SALES FORMULA AND UNDER PROPERTY-PAYROLL FORMULA BY TYPE OF BUSINESS, 1959

Number of corporations: tax liabilities

Amount (dollars)	PPS formula Total	PPS Mfg.	PPS Slg.	PP formula Total	PP Mfg.	PP Slg.
0	9	3	6	9	3	6
1-499	1		1	7		7
500-999	2		2	3		3
1,000-1,999	4	1	3	6		6
2,000-2,999	4	1	3	3	1	2
3,000-3,999	5	1	4	1	1	
4,000-4,999	2		2	2		2
5,000-7,499	8	3	5	15	6	9
7,500-9,999	8	2	6	5	2	3
10,000-14,999	14	8	6	9	4	5
15,000-24,999	13	5	8	14	7	7
25,000-49,999	9	6	3	9	7	2
50,000-99,999	9	4	5	6	3	3
100,000-149,999	4	4		10	7	3
150,000-249,999	8	5	3	3	3	
250,000-499,999	2	1	1	2	2	
500,000-999,999	1	1				
1,000,000 & over	1	1				
Totals	104	46	58	104	46	58

Number of corporations: change, PP relative to PPS formula

Percentages	Absolute Total +	Total −	Mfg. +	Mfg. −	Slg. +	Slg. −	Relative Total +	Total −	Mfg. +	Mfg. −	Slg. +	Slg. −
0	16		9		7		16		9		7	
1- 9	5	14	4	4	1	10	8	16	2	4	6	12
10- 19	2	7	1	3	1	4	4	8	2	5	2	3
20- 29	2	9	1	3	1	6	2	9	2	2		7
30- 39	4	8	3	1	1	7	5	4	5	2		2
40- 49	5	3	4	1	1	2	9	2	9	1		1
50- 59	3	2	3	1		1		8		1		7
60- 74	3	3	1	1	2	2	1	3	1	1		2
75- 99	3	3	2	1	1	2		9				9
100-149	2	10	2	1		9						
Totals	29	59	21	16	8	43	29	59	21	16	8	43

	PPS formula	PP formula
Tax liability, total:	$6,212,646	$5,680,386
Tax liability, mfg.:	4,548,921	4,502,777
Tax liability, slg.:	1,663,725	1,177,609

Source: Data obtained from individual corporations by interview and questionnaire. The tax liabilities are (1) those that were actually incurred under the property-payroll-sales formula and (2) those that would have prevailed under a property-payroll formula.

sumers are voluntarily exchanging purchasing power for things of value. If exploitation is taking place because of monopoly elements, this is a matter for antitrust action rather than recoupment by the state through taxation. Actually, these arguments are advanced in an attempt to justify a so-called "market" state (one importing more manufactured goods than it exports) in its actions to increase the size of its tax base by extending its taxing power to income created by activities outside its borders and by encouraging the location of manufacturing operations within the state.

EFFECT ON NORTH CAROLINA TAX LIABILITIES. Table XIX shows, for corporations participating in the study, the effect on their 1959 tax liabilities of a shift from the property-payroll-sales formula to a property-payroll formula, each factor weighted equally. In the aggregate these corporations would have paid 9 per cent less under a property-payroll formula, those only selling in the state 29 per cent less, and those manufacturing in the state 1 per cent less. If the largest taxpayer, which is primarily an out-of-state manufacturer, is removed, the aggregate tax liability is 3 per cent higher under the property-payroll formula, with that for manufacturing corporations increasing 21 per cent, compared with the 29 per cent decrease for selling corporations. Since some large North Carolina manufacturers who received very significant tax relief with the 1957 formula revision refused to divulge tax data for use in the study,[13] the results with the removal of this large national manufacturer are more in line with what the results would be for the whole population. It

13. The tax relief received by these corporations can be estimated by using the percentage of income taxable in North Carolina before and after the revision, which percentages are published annually by the Department of Revenue in *Stock and Bond Values,* and published net income figures.

should be kept in mind that the sample consists largely of multi-state corporations affected by formula revisions.

The distributions are probably more significant than the aggregates. While about twice as many of all of the corporations would pay less under the property-payroll formula than would pay more, a greater number of manufacturing corporations would pay more than less. Nearly half of the manufacturing corporations paying more would pay 40 to 50 per cent more, while none of the selling corporations paying more would pay as much as 20 per cent more. Over two-fifths of the selling corporations paying less would pay at least 50 per cent less, while this would be true for only an eighth of the manufacturing corporations paying less.

As expected, the manufacturing corporations that would experience a decrease in their tax liabilities under a property-payroll formula are generally national manufacturers having a small portion of their manufacturing facilities in North Carolina. The few selling corporations that would experience increased tax liabilities under this two-factor formula are strictly sellers with no manufacturing facilities anywhere (for example, a retail chain or wholesale distributor).

On the basis of data in Table XX, which excludes the largest taxpayer from the participating corporations furnishing complete data, under either the new formula or the property-payroll formula aggregate revenue is 7 to 9 per cent less than under the old formulae. The tax liabilities of manufacturing corporations would be slightly less under a property-payroll formula (relative to the old property-manufacturing cost formula), while those of selling corporations would be quite substantially less (property-payroll relative to old property-sales). Though a property-payroll formula would have differed markedly

Table XX

AGGREGATE NORTH CAROLINA INCOME TAX LIABILITIES OF
103 CORPORATIONS UNDER OLD FORMULAE, NEW
FORMULA, AND PROPERTY-PAYROLL FORMULA,
BY TYPE OF BUSINESS, 1959
(Thousands of dollars)

Classification	AGGREGATE LIABILITIES		
	Old formulae	New formula	Property-payroll formula
Total corporations.........	5,114	4,633	4,778
Manufacturing corporations.	3,698	2,969	3,601
Selling corporations........	1,416	1,664	1,178

Source: Data obtained from individual corporations by interview and questionnaire. Excluded from the corporations in Table XIX is the largest taxpayer. Excluded from the corporations in Table VIII are (1) the largest and (2) those for which tax liabilities under a property-payroll formula are not available.

from the property-payroll-sales formula in terms of effects on the tax liabilities of North Carolina manufacturers selling nationally and out-of-state manufacturers selling in North Carolina, the institution of the former instead of the latter for all corporations would have rectified the inequities associated with the old apportionment method at about the same cost in terms of revenue loss. Of course, this would not have reduced the possibility of a corporation's being taxed on over 100 per cent of its income because of the non-uniformity of apportionment formulae among the states. To correct this situation will require the action discussed in the next chapter.

Conclusion

Though the taxation of business, as well as many other things, may be questioned on theoretical grounds, the raising of public revenue by taxing corporate net income is an accepted practice. With states levying income taxes on corporations operating as a unit in the national economy, the problem of determining the portion of a corporation's unitary income attributable to a single state arises. The soundest basis for making such attribution appears to be the geographical location of the income-creating resources employed by the firm. Broadly, these are labor and property (land and capital). Therefore, the use of a formula embodying these two factors is theoretically sound. It also ranks high, relative to alternative formulae, on such criteria as simplicity, certainty, administrative and compliance costs, and effect on resource allocation and economic growth.

Inclusion of a sales factor, whatever the definition or basis of sales, cannot be economically justified under the contribution-to-income approach. A destination sales factor may be justified under the burden-of-tax approach, but justification of the approach is tenuous.

Chapter VI

Economic Analysis: Uniformity

Introduction

With business firms increasingly operating across state lines within a national economy that is becoming smaller on the communications level, the problems of interstate taxation become more acute. While problems of inter-governmental fiscal relations arise in connection with several types of taxes, this discussion is limited to the corporate income tax. The purpose of the chapter is to present the need for uniformity in the state taxation of interstate business income and to consider some methods of implementing such uniformity.

Need for Uniformity

The lack of uniformity among the corporate income tax states in their methods of taxing the income of multi-state businesses was shown in Chapter II. Variations exist with respect to allowing separate accounting, with respect to directly allocating non-unitary net income, and with respect to the formulae provided for apportioning unitary net income. The effects of these variations are several.

The most serious effect of non-uniformity is the interference with the free flow of commerce within the nation. With the divergent methods, there is to some degree, though perhaps small, a non-economic allocation of resources. The manipulations engaged in for tax purposes keep commerce from flowing as freely as it would in their

Table XXI
COMMENTS OF CORPORATIONS ON DESIRABILITY OF UNIFORMITY, BY TYPE OF BUSINESS

Comment	NUMBER OF CORPORATIONS		
	Total	Manufacturing	Selling
Favor			
With no comment..........................	23	13	10
With reason:			
Would prevent multiple taxation and minimize compliance costs.............	15	9	6
Would prevent multiple taxation..........	18	5	13
Would minimize compliance costs.........	7	2	5
Would assure equal treatment............	1	1	0
Would assure no income escapes taxation...	1	1	0
With condition:			
With special treatment in certain situations.	4	1	3
With property-payroll-sales formula.......	1	1	0
With property-payroll formula...........	1	1	0
With property-payroll-sales of property-payroll formula.......................	1	1	0
With property-sales formula.............	1	0	1
With sales included in two- or three-factor formula........................	1	1	0
With most any formula..................	1	1	0
Provided aggregate revenue of states not increased.........................	1	0	1
With comment:			
But will be difficult to achieve............	2	1	1
But will require Congressional action......	2	1	1
Even if taxpayers pay more taxes.........	1	1	0
	81	40	41
Oppose			
With no comment..........................	2	0	2
With reason:			
Would increase taxpayer's tax bill.........	1	1	0
Each state's problems different...........	1	1	0
Different formulae for different types of business required.....................	1	0	1
Separate accounting preferred...........	1	0	1
With condition:			
If NCCUSL formula used...............	1	1	0
	7	3	4
Neither position taken			
Comment:			
Will be difficult to get states to agree on sales definition.......................	2	1	1

Table XXI continued

Comment	NUMBER OF CORPORATIONS		
	Total	Manufacturing	Selling
Uniformity may be forced by Congressional action................................	1	1	0
Prefer to be taxed in only one state.......	1	1	0
Will not benefit states that need revenue...	1	0	1
	5	3	2
No answer...............................	33	14	19
Total corporations............	126	60	66

Source: Data obtained from individual corporations by interview and questionnaire.

absence. Thus non-uniformity tends to be a burden on the economy, operating as a depressant on per capita real income.

Non-uniformity is a further burden on the economy in that it causes more resources to be allocated to tax compliance and administration than would be necessary with uniform methods. Taxpayers are faced with higher record-keeping, accounting, and legal costs and the states are faced with a more difficult auditing task.

In the face of these divergent laws and interpretations, the individual taxpayer is less certain as to what his tax liability is, and competitors operating in different states and even in the same states may experience discriminatory tax treatment.

Finally, a multi-state corporation filing under the various state laws may find that more than 100 per cent or less than 100 per cent of its income is apportioned to the states in which it operates. With some states not levying corporate income taxes, most interstate corporations do not pay state income taxes on 100 per cent of their net income, but a small percentage finds more than 100 per cent of

net income subject to these taxes.[1] If all states levied
corporate income taxes, a larger percentage of corporations would be assessed on more than 100 per cent of net
income, but the net result of the divergent and over-
lapping formulae could well be that a majority of the interstate firms would declare less than 100 per cent of net
income on state income tax returns.

There is an excellent case, then, for uniformity. Furthermore, the taxpayers generally favor it. Of the participating corporations taking a position on the matter,
over 90 per cent favor uniformity, though some attach
qualifications or conditions. As shown in Table XXI,
practically all of those firms giving reasons for favoring
uniformity listed the prevention of multiple taxation
and/or the minimization of compliance costs.[2] Among the
few opponents to a uniform apportionment formula are
those who favor separate accounting or different formulae
for different types of business.

The principal obstacle to achieving uniformity is the
states themselves. Faced with the chronic problem of
finding additional revenue to finance expanded and more
expensive services, a state tends to employ the particular

1. Among 23 manufacturing corporations surveyed, Studenski and
Glasser found four with more than 100 per cent of their net income
subject to tax, but the percentages were not much above 100: 100.3
(taxed in two states); 100.5 (five states); 101.5 (two states); 103.2
(three states). (Paul Studenski and Gerald J. Glasser, "New Threat in
State Business Taxation," *Harvard Business Review*, XXXVI [November-
December, 1958] pp. 84-85.) Based on the interviews with or information received from the 126 corporations participating in this study, it is
believed that 4 out of 23 is a higher percentage (17 per cent) than exists
in the population.

2. For estimates of the relative reduction in compliance costs for 460
interstate industrial and mercantile corporations under a uniform formula,
see Albert H. Cohen, *Apportionment and Allocation Formulae and
Factors Used by States in Levying Taxes Based on or Measured by Net
Income of Manufacturing, Distributive and Extractive Corporations*
(New York: Controllership Foundation, 1954), pp. 42-49.

formula that will give it the most revenue. For example, an industrial state is apt to use the origin basis for sales in its formula, while an agrarian state is apt to use the destination basis. The sales destination basis is attractive not only to the state that is a net importer of manufactured goods but also to the state that hopes to attract industry by giving tax relief to local manufacturers selling nationally. There is no formula that could be universally adopted without affecting differently the revenues of the individual states.[3]

Implementation

The general desirability of uniformity in the state taxation of business income can hardly be gainsaid, but reaching agreement on the particular formula to be used is indeed another matter.[4] The initiative in implementing a

3. For an estimate of the effect on state revenues of three different formulae (property-payroll-sales, with sales defined differently: negotiation, origin, delivery), see Council of State Governments, *Report of Survey of Effects on State Revenues of Various Proposed Uniform Apportionment Formulas* (Chicago: CSG [May, 1956], mimeographed). The estimates were based on 125 usable replies received from 650 concerns to which questionnaires were sent. It was indicated that the adoption of any one of the formulae by all states would have little effect on the revenues of most states, but might produce significant increases or serious losses for a few. Twenty-nine of the 125 firms paid North Carolina income taxes in 1954; 33 would have paid, if a uniform property-payroll-sales (delivery) formula had been in effect, 28.8 per cent less. This estimate was about four times greater than the actual relative loss experienced when North Carolina adopted this formula in 1957.

4. For discussions of possible solutions to the problem, see George D. Braden, "Cutting the Gordian Knot of Interstate Taxation," *Ohio State Law Journal*, XVIII (Winter, 1957), pp. 57-68; Congressional *Hearings* cited in n. 25, p. 15; Fred L. Cox, "The Impact of Recent Supreme Court Decisions on State Taxation of Interstate Commerce," *Proceedings of the NTA* (1959), pp. 441-45; Cox, "Uniformity in Apportionment of Multistate Income: Its Need and Proper Method of Achievement," *Taxes*, XXXIII (July, 1955), pp. 526-31; John Dane, Jr., "Breck and Panhandle: Impracticality of Judicial Standards for Interstate Taxation," *Journal of Taxation*, VIII (May, 1958), pp. 278-80; Dane, "Small Business Looks at Public Law 86-272 in the Perspective of its Alternatives," *Virginia Law Review*, XLVI (October, 1960), pp. 1190-1211;

uniform apportionment formula might be taken by the Court, the states, or the federal Congress. It has already been seen (Chapter II) that Court actions, which involve specific issues as they arise, do not result in a uniform formula. This leaves as possible avenues of reform, then, the several states and Congress.

If the states take the initiative, uniformity must be achieved through an interstate compact, which requires the consent of Congress, or through the adoption by all the corporate income tax states of a uniform formula. Either approach would require voluntary agreement on the part of the several states to the particular formula,[5] and experience in this area over the past half century leads to the conclusion that such voluntary agreement is next to impossible (Chapter II).

If Congress takes the initiative, several alternative

Martin Drazen, "Recent Trends in State Taxation of Interstate Commerce," *Taxes*, XXXIV (April, 1956), pp. 286-90; Jerome R. Hellerstein, "The Power of Congress to Restrict State Taxation of Interstate Commerce," *Journal of Taxation*, XII (May, 1960), pp. 302-5; Jerome R. Hellerstein and Edmund B. Hennefeld, "State Taxation in a National Economy," *Harvard Law Review*, LIV (April, 1941), pp. 949-76; George H. Kitendaugh, "Possibilities for Interstate Cooperation in the Area of Allocation Formulas," *Federal-State-Local Tax Correlation* (Princeton: Tax Institute, 1954), pp. 205-10; Leonard E. Kust, "State Taxation of Interstate Income: New Dimensions of an Old Problem," *Tax Executive*, XII (October, 1959), pp. 45-67; Arthur D. Lynn, Jr., "Formula Apportionment of Corporate Income for State Purposes: Natura Non Facit Saltum," *Ohio State Law Journal*, XVIII (Winter, 1957), pp. 84-104; Paul Studenski, "State Taxation of Interstate Commerce," *Tax Review*, XX (July, 1959), pp. 25-28; Studenski, "The Need for Federal Curbs on State Taxes on Interstate Commerce: An Economist's Viewpoint," *Virginia Law Review*, XLVI (October, 1960), pp. 1121-49; John A. Wilkie, *Allocation of Multistate Income Under State Corporate Net Income Taxes* (Ann Arbor: University Microfilms, Inc., 1957), pp. 456-95.

5. Of course, a compact among a majority of the states might be combined with Congressional prohibition of all formulae other than the compact formula to force all states to use the compact formula. For a detailed presentation of this state-federal approach, see Wilkie, *Allocation of Multistate Income*, pp. 481-90.

courses are available. One, which is a somewhat in-between course, is to establish an administrative agency that has as its function prodding the states into co-operating. This would interfere practically not at all with state taxing powers, but the achievement of uniformity would be a slow process, if accomplished ever.

Another possible course would be for the federal government to levy the only corporate income tax and to share part of the revenue with the states on the basis of origin or to make grants-in-aid. Many pros and cons dealing with administrative efficiency, compliance costs, control over spending, and other matters could be enumerated here, but this course would eliminate the problem rather than implement a uniform formula.

Two other courses that Congress might follow are similar in that in each case a uniform formula would be stipulated. Under its taxing power, Congress could institute a credit against the federal corporate income tax for state income taxes, up to a certain maximum, paid to states employing the approved method of apportionment. The corporate income tax states would be "forced" to adopt the conditions laid down by Congress; these conditions might include, in addition to a stipulated formula, use of the federal definition of taxable income and even central administration of the tax. A principal objection to the tax credit approach is that it would "force" the fourteen states that have not chosen to tax corporate net income to do so. Since the object of Congressional action would be to establish uniform apportionment methods among the corporate income tax states and not to induce all states to tax corporate net income at a certain minimum rate, the tax credit approach is rejected in favor of Congressional action under its interstate commerce power.

Under the commerce clause, Congress possesses the power to define the extent to which states may tax interstate commerce without adversely interfering with the national economic welfare. Congress could simply stipulate the apportionment formula and the tax base a state must use in taxing net income earned in interstate commerce. Uniformity would be implemented immediately and interference with state taxing powers would be slight. Of course, Congress could possibly go further and require central administration, so that a firm would file one return with the Internal Revenue Service to cover its federal and state tax liabilities.[6]

If uniformity is to be achieved without undue delay and without undue interference with state taxing powers, the appropriate course of action would appear to be a federal statute stipulating the tax base and apportionment formula. In the opinion of the author, the tax base should be the federal definition of taxable income, with some adjustments allowed,[7] and the formula should be the property-payroll formula.

The institution of a uniform formula will increase the revenues of some states and reduce those of others, depending upon the formulae involved and the nature of business activity within the state. For example, replacing a property-payroll-destination sales formula with a property-payroll formula in a "market" state would reduce revenues; in a "manufacturing" state this would increase revenues. Were such not the case, the states might have agreed on a uniform formula long ago. However, the

6. A state tax administrator has proposed such central administration, pointing out that the states "could contract with the Federal Government to administer their taxes for them much more reasonably than they could do so themselves" (Dixwell L. Pierce, "State Taxes Not Business Barriers," *National Tax Journal*, XIII [September, 1960], p. 239).

7. For example, an adjustment would take care of the deductibility or non-deductibility of federal income taxes among the states.

ill effects of non-uniformity are more serious from the political economy viewpoint than would be the revenue changes. As pointed out above, the lack of uniformity operates as a burden on the national economy. The immediate changes in state revenues accompanying the lifting of this burden may be less than anticipated, as was the case in North Carolina in 1957, and would certainly not be great relative to total tax revenues;[8] and for many states the losses may be transitory owing to a faster growth in their tax bases with the burden lifted. Furthermore, with a uniform property-payroll formula, the losses to a large degree would be accounted for by the elimination of the taxation of income created by resources lying outside the state experiencing the loss. If some states do not possess the ability to provide certain services of nationwide significance at the desirable level, federal grants-in-aid constitute a more appropriate remedy, economically, than does state taxation extraterritorially.

Conclusion

On the side of minimizing the interference of taxation with the most efficient utilization of resources, it is desirable that states employ a uniform method of apportioning interstate income for tax purposes. Since it appears very unlikely that the states will ever voluntarily agree to the same method, under its commerce power Congress

8. For the importance of the corporate income tax for each state, see data published annually by the U.S. Department of Commerce in *Compendium of State Government Finances in* [year]. In 1960 the states obtained 6.5 per cent of their tax revenue from the corporate net income tax. For only ten (California, Connecticut, Delaware, Minnesota, New York, North Carolina, Oregon, Pennsylvania, Virginia, and Wisconsin) did this tax account for at least 10 per cent of total tax revenue. (*Compendium* for 1960, p. 13.) Thus for a majority of the corporate net income tax states a 10 per cent change in corporate net income tax revenue would mean a change of less than 1 per cent in total tax revenue.

should establish, as a condition to state taxation of net income from interstate commerce, the method of apportionment.

Though a uniform method embodying almost any apportionment formula would in large measure correct the ill effects of non-uniformity, the formula that would go farthest in rectifying the situation is a two-factor property-payroll formula.

Chapter VII

Conclusion

The North Carolina Experience

THE PROBLEM. With the method of apportionment used since the depression, North Carolina faced the problem that its tax structure appeared to be relatively harsh on multi-state business and thus was possibly a deterrent to economic development. Three features embodied in the apportionment method gave the impression that the state was bent on extracting the constitutional maximum of taxes from multi-state businesses and was in some situations taxing income not economically attributable to the state. These were the separate treatment of domestic and foreign corporations, the former not being allowed to apportion income by formula; the discriminatory treatment of foreign corporations, the formula applicable depending upon the principal business of the corporation within North Carolina; and, in the statute, no separate allocation of non-unitary income.

Combined with the relatively high tax rate and the non-deductibility of federal income taxes, these features gave North Carolina the reputation of being a "high tax" state. As the interstate operations of businesses increased, there was mounting pressure for tax relief. With the increased demands for a revised method of apportionment unsatisfied by the provision for administrative relief in special cases, a Tax Study Commission was established primarily to study the apportionment method. Its recom-

mendations concerning revision of the method were
adopted with little opposition in the legislature and with
little disturbance of the public's apathy. Factors accounting for this were the tremendous popular support enjoyed
by the Governor, who had publicized tax revision and industrial development as major parts of his program; the
stature of the Commission members, who were men of
prestige representing different interests and geographical
areas; and the increased willingness of the legislature to
amend the tax laws. In addition, the legislature was
maneuvered into a position where to reject the proposed
revision would place the state in the position of stating
practically officially that it was a poor business location
with regard to taxation.

THE CHANGE. Under the revised apportionment method
the inequities existing under the old method were largely
removed by giving equal treatment to domestic and
foreign corporations, by applying the same formula to
all multi-state businesses, and by separately allocating
non-unitary income. The Tax Review Board may allow
special treatment, for example, separate accounting, in
cases where the statutory property-payroll-sales formula
is found to be unreasonable.

It must be emphasized that the inequities were corrected not by the particular apportionment formula
adopted but by eliminating the discriminatory treatment
of corporations. In fact, the property-payroll-sales formula may be questioned on equity grounds inasmuch as the
destination sales factor, under the contribution-to-income
approach to apportionment, allows some domestic industry income attributable to the state to escape taxation,
while some income not economically attributable to the
state is taxed.

THE EFFECTS. (1) *State revenue.* The reduction in

corporate income tax revenue occasioned by the revision at its inception was 7.5 per cent, or about half the amount predicted by the Commission. Though other factors such as sample representation, Commission caution, and the 1957-1958 recession entered the picture, the principal reason for the difference between the expected loss and the actual loss was the serious underestimation of the sales factor in the calculation of the estimate. This same factor also largely accounts for the fact that a greater proportion of corporations than anticipated by the Commission experienced tax increases. Corporate income tax revenue has continued to be less than it would have been had the law not been revised. However, the corporate income tax due North Carolina as a percentage of corporate profits before taxes in the nation has remained amazingly stable. This may indicate that industrial growth has offset the effects of the formula revision, but the formula revision apparently has had little effect on location decisions.

(2) *Individual corporate tax liabilities.* The revision had no effect on the tax liabilities of 94 per cent of the corporations filing returns, primarily because they had no taxable income or did not engage in multi-state business. Tax liabilities of 3.8 per cent of the corporations were decreased and those of 2.2 per cent were increased. For a large portion of the affected corporations, the changes in tax liabilities were relatively small, but some experienced very significant changes. The larger share of the substantial decreases went to North Carolina manufacturers selling nationally, while out-of-state manufacturers selling in North Carolina experienced most of the greater increases. As groups, firms manufacturing in North Carolina received a reduction in taxes, while firms principally selling in the state experienced an increase. Almost completely responsible for the decrease for manufacturing firms was the

inclusion of the destination sales factor in the apportionment formula, and largely responsible for the increase for selling firms was the substitution of the destination sales factor for the through offices sales factor. For both manufacturing and selling corporations, there appears to have been a slight tendency since 1957 for the larger relative decreases to become fewer and the larger relative increases to become more numerous.

(3) *Industrial development.* The Commission was hopeful that reduction of the apparent harshness in the North Carolina tax structure would accelerate economic development in the state. In light of the minor role played by the tax factor in the location of economic activity, as found in this and other studies, it is doubtful that the changes are exerting much effect in this direction. This doubt is confirmed by the testimony of 33 major firms that located or proposed the location of new or expanded facilities in North Carolina during the three years following the revision. In only one case was the revision influential. For 150 firms participating in this study, location decisions of three had been influenced by the formula revision, but only one claimed it to be the decisive factor. In fact, very few firms regard state and local taxes to be a major factor in the location of economic activity.

(4) *Revenue behavior.* It appears that under the revised formula corporate tax collections are cyclically more unstable than before. Primarily responsible for this is probably the destination sales factor.

(5) *Reaction of taxpayers.* A majority of the firms participating in the study is satisfied with the revised formula. In general, the satisfied received tax relief and the dissatisfied experienced tax increases.

CONCLUSION 113

Economic Aspects

DEVELOPMENT OF IDEAS. With state taxation of the net income of corporations operating as units in the national economy, there exists the problem of determining the portion of a corporation's unitary income attributable to a single state. In the development of ideas concerning the proper method of apportioning unitary net income, there is considerable diversity, part of it accounted for by differences in theories but a greater part by practical, political considerations. It is generally agreed that the formula method is ordinarily superior to separate accounting in apportioning unitary net income, but the particular formula to be used is not a settled issue.

The National Tax Association committee presenting the model state and local tax plan over forty years ago envisioned no serious difficulty in determining the proportion of income earned in each state by an interstate concern. However, the two-factor property-business formula originally recommended for mercantile and manufacturing businesses did not win universal approval, and a subsequent committee recommended in 1933 the three-factor Massachusetts formula on the grounds that uniformity is preferable to scientific accuracy. Succeeding committees agreed that the property-payroll-sales formula was most likely to be universally adopted, but each made refinements in the definitions of the three factors, especially the sales factor.

Meanwhile, the National Conference of Commissioners on Uniform State Laws drafted a uniform act incorporating the property-payroll-sales formula, presenting it in 1957. Again, the feature giving rise to most of the controversy is the sales factor.

Though the general development has been in the direction of a property-payroll-sales formula with a destination basis sales factor, other proposals have been made. Apportionment of income on the basis of expenses incurred in each state and elimination of the property factor from the formula have been suggested, but most serious attention, at least by economists, is given to a two-factor property-payroll formula.

A FORMULA. An apportionment formula might be developed by either of two approaches: burden-of-tax approach or contribution-to-income approach. If the distribution of the burden of the corporate income tax were known, it would be possible to work out an apportionment formula based on the location of the individuals bearing that burden. In essence, the states would be attempting to collect revenue from their citizens via the corporations. Since it would not be so accurate or precise and would not permit the control over distributive justice as would taxing the individuals directly under individual income and sales taxes, such a formula can hardly be justified. Though it is theoretically more sound than the widely used property-payroll-sales formula in that it may justifiably include a sales factor, it possesses no practical advantages.

Under the contribution-to-income approach, there are two alternative attacks: apportionment of net income on the basis of the geographical location of the sources of business profit or apportionment on the basis of the geographical location of the factors of production creating the total income (output). The former would be practically impossible, for it would entail ferreting out and locating geographically the sources of pure and monopoly profits and the implicit costs. Even if it could be accomplished, the results would vary immensely among industries and among firms within the same industry. The latter attack, however, appears particularly relevant in light of the propensity to treat corporate income taxes as costs, all of which must be covered by income (output) for a firm to continue in business. Since in our fairly competitive economy the best indication of the contributions of the various means is the amount of money spent for them, the appropriate basis for apportioning a firm's net income among the states should be the distribution of its expenditures: a simple expense formula. Theoretically, it is sound; practically, though, there are some problems in the areas of compliance and administration, and it would be a sharp departure from the formulae now in use.

In the interest of simplicity, the expense formula may be streamlined to consist of the broad categories of the productive factors, whose contributions to income (output) are indicated by readily available and fairly easily apportioned data. Payroll data furnish the amount spent on the labor factor, and property values indicate the value of services performed by land and capital factors. The labor-property weight could logically be 3 to 1, in accordance with the national income accounts, and this would assure to labor "full weight," which is essential in the area of selling activities in which the payroll factor may not "follow" the property factor.

The property-payroll formula is theoretically sound and is also superior to alternative formulae on such criteria as simplicity, certainty, administrative and compliance costs, and effect on resource allocation and economic growth. Inclusion of a sales factor, whatever the basis of sales, cannot be economically justified under the contribution-to-income approach; and the sales factor is the one responsible for most of the practical difficulties.

If North Carolina had adopted the property-payroll formula when it eliminated the discriminatory treatment of corporations in 1957, the cost in terms of revenue loss would have been about the same as it was with adoption of the property-payroll-sales formula. And it appears that both manufacturing and selling corporations, as groups, would have received reduced tax liabilities rather than one group only. Most important, the state would not have adopted a formula that tends to allow income created within the state to escape taxation and to submit to taxation income created outside the state.

UNIFORMITY. The case for uniform apportionment methods among the corporate income tax states is a very strong one. Foremost, non-uniformity is a burden on the economy in that it interferes with the most efficient utilization of resources: it results in some non-economic allocation of resources and in an unnecessarily large amount of resources being used in tax compliance and administration. Furthermore, non-uniformity leaves room for uncertainty in tax liabilities and for discriminatory tax treatment. Finally, it results in both multiple taxation and under taxation, but probably more often the latter.

Most taxpayers faced with the task of paying corporate income taxes in more than one state favor uniformity, but the states have never been able to agree on a particular formula. With each state prone to use the formula most favorable to it in respect either to revenue or industry-attracting, voluntary agreement by all states on one formula is very unlikely. Neither are the actions of the Court, which deals with specific issues as they arise, very likely to result in a uniform formula. The avenue of reform, then, is Congressional action.

Congress could levy the only corporate income tax, sharing the revenue with the states, but this would eliminate the problem rather than implement a uniform formula. It could "force" the states to adopt a uniform formula by using the tax credit device, but this would also "force" all states to adopt a corporate income tax. Implementation of uniformity with minimum interference with state taxing powers can be achieved by Congressional exercise of the commerce power to stipulate the conditions under which a state may tax net income earned in interstate commerce. These conditions would include the definition of taxable income and the apportionment method. Ideally, the former would be related to the definition for federal tax purposes and the latter would embody the property-payroll formula.

Constitutional and Statutory Aspects

CONSTITUTIONAL. In interpreting the commerce and due process clauses as they apply to state taxation of commerce, the Court's position has vacillated, and it has made distinctions based on labels rather than on economics. Under the "direct-indirect" burdens test, which held sway from the 1880's to the 1930's, state taxes found to be a direct burden on interstate commerce were held invalid. In 1938 this test was replaced by the pragmatic "cumulative burdens" test, which allowed state taxation of interstate commerce provided the interstate commerce was not subject to the risk of multiple taxation not borne by local commerce. Eight years later, however, the old test was resurrected. It has been perpetuated in cases since then, along with a much-revised "cumulative burdens" test.

While a state may not levy a privilege tax measured by net income on a foreign corporation engaged in exclusively interstate commerce or on the interstate portion of net income of one engaged in both interstate and intrastate commerce, it may levy a fairly apportioned, nondiscriminatory net income tax on a foreign corporation, assuming sufficient nexus, even if all of the income is derived from interstate commerce. Though the only difference in the two taxes be the name (privilege *v.* net income), this distinction is maintained by the Court. Of course, a state may legally, if not politically, tax the entire net income of a domestic corporation, regardless of whether some of the income is earned outside the state.

STATUTORY. There has been a definite trend towards a three-factor statutory formula comprised of property, payroll (or manufacturing cost), and sales. However, with the various definitions of factors employed by different states, uniformity does not exist to the degree that may be suggested by the number of states using the three-factor formula. Furthermore, variations exist in the treatment of non-unitary income and the allowance of separate accounting.

Further Reform

To bring our tax structure into conformity with our twentieth-century national economy, many improvements along the line of the one proposed here may have to be made. The economy is interdependent on a national scale and state boundaries become progressively dimmer economically. It is essential that they not encourage a non-economic allocation of resources; consequently, to require uniformity in income apportionment as proposed here is a step in that direction. Congressional action with respect to other taxes may be required. Congress must decide whether to take one step at a time or several at once, but it should certainly in a forthright, statesmanlike manner do one or the other.

Appendix

Index

NUMBER OF CORPORATIONS AND AMOUNT OF CHANGE IN TAX LIABILITIES, BY TYPE OF BUSINESS AND TYPE OF CORPORATION, 1957

(Amounts in thousands of dollars)

Type of business		NUMBER OF CORPORATIONS AND AMOUNT OF CHANGE IN TAX LIABILITIES								
		All corporations			Domestic corporations			Foreign corporations		
		Increase	Decrease	Net loss	Increase	Decrease	Net loss	Increase	Decrease	Net loss
Agricultural and extractive	Number:	5	10	15	2	2	4	3	8	11
	Amount:	3	14	12	*	13	12	3	2	(1)
Construction	Number:	17	24	41	12	22	34	5	2	7
	Amount:	7	16	9	3	14	11	4	2	(2)
Finance	Number:	0	2	2	0	1	1	0	1	1
	Amount:	0	*	*	0	*	*	0	*	*
Manufacturing Food and feed	Number:	11	23	34	4	7	11	7	16	23
	Amount:	4	72	68	1	36	35	3	36	33
Forest products	Number:	10	18	28	2	9	11	8	9	17
	Amount:	23	395	372	1	49	48	22	346	324
Mineral, chemical, metal	Number:	7	14	21	1	4	5	6	10	16
	Amount:	14	18	4	7	7	(*)	6	11	4
Textile	Number:	14	58	72	0	17	17	14	41	55
	Amount:	425	1,213	789	0	837	837	425	376	(49)
Tobacco[a]	Number:	3	7	10						
	Amount:	18	1,917	1,899						
Other	Number:	15	42	57	1	6	7	14	36	50
	Amount:	49	482	433	*	65	65	49	417	368
Total manufacturing	Number:	60	162	222	8	44	52	52	118	170
	Amount:	532	4,097	3,565	9	996	987	523	3,100	2,577

		1	2	3	4	5	6	7	8	9
Miscellaneous	Number:	1	3	4	0	1	1	1	2	3
	Amount:	*	1	1	0	*	*	*	1	1
Public utility	Number:	1	6	7	1	5	6	0	1	1
	Amount:	*	122	122	*	122	122	0	*	*
Recreation and amusement	Number:	7	2	9	0	1	1	7	1	8
	Amount:	2	1	(*)	0	*	*	2	1	(1)
Service	Number:	25	34	59	7	11	18	18	23	41
	Amount:	27	8	(19)	1	2	1	26	6	(21)
Trade Automotive	Number:	22	41	63	1	1	2	21	40	61
	Amount:	497	69	(428)	*	*	*	497	69	(428)
Beverage, food, drug	Number:	52	92	144	2	6	8	50	86	136
	Amount:	73	42	(31)	*	1	1	7	40	32
Equipment and supplies	Number:	102	164	266	6	15	21	96	149	245
	Amount:	78	183	105	2	4	2	76	179	102
General merchandise	Number:	49	58	107	3	8	11	46	50	96
	Amount:	27	69	42	*	2	2	27	67	40
Unclassified	Number:	27	31	58	5	1	6	22	30	52
	Amount:	14	7	(8)	1	*	(1)	13	7	(6)
Total trade	Number:	252	386	638	17	31	48	235	355	590
	Amount:	689	369	(319)	3	8	5	685	361	(324)
Total manufacturing and trade	Number:	312	548	860	25	75	100	287	473	760
	Amount:	1,221	4,466	3,245	13	1,004	992	1,208	3,462	2,253
Grand total	Number:	368	629	997	47	118	165	321	511	832
	Amount:	1,259	4,628	3,369	16	1,155	1,139	1,243	3,474	2,230

Source: Worksheets of the North Carolina Department of Tax Research, Raleigh.
* Less than $500.
ª Data shown only for all corporations to preserve anonymity of corporations.

Index

Cooley decision, 11
Corporate income tax, constitutionality of, 9-16, 42; tax deductibility of, 36, 47, 80, 90, 106n, 109; and property tax, 39n; incidence of, 83-84, 86-88; applied to various concepts of profit, 89-90; importance of to states, 107
Corporate profits, related to taxes due N.C., 78-79, 111
Corporations, participation of in study, 5-6; selection of, 6-7; number participating, 7-8; number affected by formula revision, 55-56, 80; effect of formula on tax liabilities of, 55-59, 62-68, 111-12; as tax avoidance instrument, 61-63, 82-83; reaction of to revised formula, 70-72, 122; position on uniformity, 100-2, 116
Correlation analysis, as study method, 72
Costs, administrative, 3, 24, 92, 98, 101, 105, 115; compliance, 3, 24, 92, 98, 101, 102, 105, 115; explicit, 88-90; implicit, 88-90
Council of State Governments, 20
Cumulative burdens test, 12-14, 117
Currie decision, 15

Delaware, 107n
Destination basis sales factor, reasons recommended by NCCUSL, 22-23; arguments for by N.C. Tax Study Commission, 43; and burden-of-tax approach, 88; evaluated, 93-95; mentioned, 72, 113-14
Direct allocation, use by states, 3, 31, 85; and revenue estimate, 55
Direct-indirect burdens test, 12-14, 117
Discriminatory tax treatment, based on corporate domicile, 35, 82, 109; based on nature of business, 35-36, 82, 109; and non-uniformity, 101, 116

District of Columbia, 3
Domestic corporations, jurisdiction of state to tax, 14, 16, 118; tax treatment of, 32-33, 35, 40-41, 48; effect of formula revision on, 55-68 *passim*
Due process clause, limitation on state tax power, 9; interpreted by Court, 9-15, 117-18; relation to apportionment method, 11, 14; and nexus, 16; mentioned, 4

Economic development, 92, 98, 115. *See also* Industrial development
Economic profit. *See* Pure profit
Economy, interdependent, 3, 118
Equity, in distribution of tax burden, 84, 87
Equity capital, 28, 87, 88
Excess profits tax, 47
Executive salaries, and payroll factor, 42-43
Expense formula, proposal, 23-24, 114; described, 91; evaluated, 91, 115
Exploitation, 93-95
Extraterritorial taxation, 26-27, 107, 116

Factors of production, and income or output, 91, 114; indicator of contribution of, 91, 115
Foreign corporations, jurisdiction of state to tax, 9-14, 16, 117-18; tax treatment of, 32-34, 35-36, 40-41, 48; effects of formula revision on, 55-68 *passim*
Formula revision, factors accounting for adoption, 46-47, 110
Franchise tax, 68
Full cost pricing, 83

Georgia, 29n
Grants-in-aid, and implementation of uniformity, 105; as remedy, 107
Gross income tax, legally distinguished, 14
Gross receipts, factor, 17, 19n; formula, 32, 40

INDEX

125

Hans Rees' Sons, Inc., 33
Hawaii, 31n
Hodges, Luther H., 46
Hypothetical tax bill approach, as study method, 72

Imperfect competition, 83
Incidence, of corporate income tax, 83-84, 86-88
Income, *ex ante* and *ex post*, 88; real per capita, 101
Income Tax Committee, report of, 39-40
Individual income tax, 63, 68, 86, 114
Individual income tax revenue, effect of formula revision on, 68-69
Individuals, effect of formula revision on tax liabilities of, 68-71
Industrial development, effect of formula revision on, 6, 8, 53, 72-79, 81, 111, 112; and tax structure, 34-35, 109; and formula revision, 40-41, 44, 110; factors in location decisions, 74-78; and apportionment formulae, 92, 103, 107, 115
Inflationary trends, 83
Innovations, 88
Intangibles tax, 63, 68
Intangibles tax revenue, effect of formula revision on, 68-69; distribution, 69n
Internal Revenue Service, 106
Interstate business operations, tax problems precipitated by, 3
Interstate commerce, concurrent v. exclusive power to regulate, 11-12; multiple taxation of, 12. *See also* Commerce clause, Commerce power
Interstate compact, 104
Interview, as study method, 6-8, 72
Intrafirm transfer price, 24

Jurisdiction, of state to tax, 3, 9-14, 20, 44, 117-18

Legislators, and formula revision, 45-46, 47
Limited jurisdiction, and tax shifting, 84, 86-87
Location decisions. *See* Industrial development

Manpower, as location factor, 73
Manufacturing corporations, tax treatment of, 32-34, 35, 40-42; effect of formula revision on 55-68 *passim*, 111-12; and property-payroll formula, 95-97, 116
Manufacturing space, as location factor, 75
Market, as location factor, 73, 75
Marshall, John, 11, 12
Massachusetts, 31n
Massachusetts formula, 18, 113
Minnesota, 107n
Model plan for state and local taxation, 17-18
Momentum of early start, as location factor, 75
Montana, 29n
Moody's *Industrial Manual*, 6
Motivational research, as study method, 72
Multiple taxation, 12, 97, 101-2, 116

National Conference of Commissioners on Uniform State Laws, proposed formula, 21-23, 113
National Tax Association, formula proposals, 17-21, 113
Net income, definition problem, 3; apportionment problem, 3; jurisdiction problem, 3
New Jersey, 31n
New York, 33, 107n
New York City, 7
Nexus, and tax constitutionality, 16, 117
Nondiscriminatory tax, and tax constitutionality, 15-16, 117
Non-unitary income, tax treatment of, 36, 40-42, 47-48, 109. *See also* Direct allocation

AUTHOR-TITLE

Britton, Floyd E., 27n
Brown-Forman Distillers Corp. v.
    Collector of Revenue, 16n
Brown v. Maryland, 11n
Bullock, Charles J., 17n
"Burden of the Corporate Income
    Tax," 83n

Carbert, Leslie E., 38n, 53n
Case of the State Freight Tax, 11n
Case of the State Tax on Foreign-
    Held Bonds, 10n
Charlotte News, 45n
Charlotte Observer, 44n, 45n, 46n
Cohen, Albert H., 24n, 85n, 102n
Comments on the Allocation Form-
    ulas . . . , 33n
"Comparison of North Carolina
    . . . ," 39n
Compendium of State Government
    Finances, 107n
Concord Tribune, 45n
Congressional Record, 16n
Conlon, Charles F., 21n, 23n, 27n
"Constitutional Law," 10n
Cooley v. Board of Wardens, 11
"Corporate Tax Allocation in Wis-
    consin," 28n
"Corporate Tax Reduction," 46n
Corporation Income Taxes, 39n
Council of State Governments, 103n
Cox, Fred L., 20n, 21n, 27n, 103n
Crandall v. Nevada, 11n
"Current State of Profit Theory,"
    89n
"Cutting the Gordian Knot . . . ,"
    103n

Dane, John, Jr., 10n, 21n, 103n
Davis, Richard M., 89n
"Death of a Salesman," 9n
Directory of Manufacturing Firms,
    6
DiSanto v. Pennsylvania, 12n
"Drafts of . . . Income Tax Acts,"
    17n
Drazen, Martin, 104n
Due, John F., 72n, 88n
Durham Herald, 44n, 45n
Durham Sun, 45n

"Economic Aspects of . . . Appor-
    tionment . . . ," 25n
Edmonds, Franklin S., 19n
Effects of Taxation on . . . Loca-
    tion, 72n
"Elimination of Double Taxation
    . . . ," 23n
ET&WNC Transp. Co. v. Currie,
    4n, 13n, 15n
Expenditure Tax, 84n

"Factors . . . in Per Capita In-
    come," 38n-39n
"Federal Limitations on State Tax-
    ation . . . ," 25n, 27n
"Federal Taxes . . . and . . . Re-
    turn on Investment . . . ," 83n
Federal-State-Local Tax Correla-
    tion, 27n
"Final Report . . . on Tax Situs
    and Allocation," 19n
Floyd, Joe S., Jr., 72n
Ford, Robert S., 24n, 25n
Ford Motor Co. v. Beauchamp, 11n
"Formula Apportionment of . . .
    Income . . . ," 104n
"Form Versus Substance," 10n
Freeman v. Hewit, 13n

Gastonia Gazette, 45n
"Generalized Uncertainty Theory of
    Profit, A," 88n
General Statutes of North Carolina,
    8n, 40n
Gerstenberg, Charles W., 18n, 25n,
    29
Glasser, Gerald J., 102n
Gray, Otha L., 10n
Greensboro Daily News, 44n, 45n
Groves, H. M., 72n
Guthrie, Paul, 38n
Gwin, White, & Prince, Inc. v.
    Henneford, 13n

Haber, W., 72n
Hamilton, C. Horace, 39n
Han, P. B., 83n
Hans Rees' Sons, Inc. v. North
    Carolina, 4n, 11n, 14n, 33n
Harriss, C. Lowell, 25n, 26n, 28n,
    84n